More praise for *The Agility Factor*

"All business leaders who deal with a rapidly changing business environment must read this book. You will learn how you can make your organization a winner in the 'creative destruction' game while continuing to financially outperform your rivals."

—Tony Petrella, consultant; and founding partner of Block-Petrella-Weisbords

"*The Agility Factor* is an outstanding research-based guide to creating adaptable, high-performance organizations. A great read for managers, consultants, and scholars."

—Warren Bennis, Distinguished Professor of Business Administration, and founding chairman of The Leadership Institute, University of Southern California

"Clear a space on your bookshelf and make room for *The Agility Factor*! It is a unique and useable approach to change and leading through difficult management challenges. Every human resource in your organization will find their way to engagement and focused results through use of these principles."

—Sue McNab, vice president and CHRO, PEMCO Insurance

"For two decades, Chris Worley and Ed Lawler have been the most compelling voices calling for adaptive, healthy organizations. Now with Tom Williams, they present a beautifully researched and clear case for the success criteria for organizations in today's hyper-competitive landscape."

—Foster W. Mobley, founder and CEO, FMG Leading

"Worley, Williams, and Lawler have unraveled the nugget of sustained organizational performance. In an increasingly volatile, uncertain, complex, and ambiguous business context, organizations maintain superior performance by building the capability of agility. Agile corporations strategize, perceive, test, and implement faster than competitors and consistent with market changes. Their work is a marvelous integration of innovative ideas, sound research, and relevant actions."

—Dave Ulrich, professor, Ross School of Business, University of Michigan; and partner, The RBL Group

"The half-life of a distinctive, coherent strategy is shrinking in today's dynamic marketplace. Leading organizations make up for this with agility as they sense and respond to rapid changes before their competitors. This becomes the new competitive advantage for the twenty-first century."

—R. Andrew Clyde, president and CEO, Murphy USA Inc.

The Jossey-Bass
Business & Management Series

THE AGILITY FACTOR

Building Adaptable Organizations
for Superior Performance

CHRISTOPHER G. WORLEY
THOMAS WILLIAMS
EDWARD E. LAWLER III

Foreword by James O'Toole

JB JOSSEY-BASS™
A Wiley Brand

Copyright © 2014 by John Wiley & Sons, Inc. All rights reserved.

Published by Jossey-Bass
A Wiley Brand
One Montgomery Street, Suite 1200, San Francisco, CA 94104-4594—www.josseybass.com

Jossey-Bass books and products are available through most bookstores. To contact Jossey-Bass directly call our Customer Care Department within the U.S. at 800-956-7739, outside the U.S. at 317-572-3986, or fax 317-572-4002.

Wiley publishes in a variety of print and electronic formats and by print-on-demand. Some material included with standard print versions of this book may not be included in e-books or in print-on-demand. If this book refers to media such as a CD or DVD that is not included in the version you purchased, you may download this material at http://booksupport.wiley.com. For more information about Wiley products, visit www.wiley.com.

Library of Congress Cataloging-in-Publication Data

Worley, Christopher G.
   The agility factor: building adaptable organizations for superior performance/
Christopher G. Worley, Thomas Williams, Edward E. Lawler, III; foreword by James O'Toole.
      pages cm
   Includes bibliographical references and index.
   ISBN 978-1-118-82137-4 (hardback); ISBN 978-1-118-82141-1 (ebk); 978-1-118-82139-8 (ebk)
   1. Organizational change–Management.   2. Organizational effectiveness.   I. Williams, Thomas.   II. Lawler, Edward E.   III. Title.
   HD58.8.W683 2014
   658.4'06–dc23

                                                     2014019132

Printed in the United States of America
FIRST EDITION
HB Printing   10 9 8 7 6 5 4 3 2 1

CONTENTS

Foreword by James O'Toole   ix

Preface   xiii

CHAPTER 1 SEARCHING FOR SUSTAINED
PERFORMANCE   1

CHAPTER 2 ORGANIZING FOR AGILITY   25

CHAPTER 3 STRATEGIZING AND PERCEIVING   53

CHAPTER 4 TESTING AND IMPLEMENTING   83

CHAPTER 5 TRANSFORMING TO AGILITY   111

Afterword: Some Reflections on Agility   139

Notes   147

About The Authors   157

Acknowledgments   159

Index   161

FOREWORD

A century ago, a young retailer named James Cash Penney explained to one of his managers how he planned to reorganize their company in new and untried ways, all of which were designed to empower the managers of the small chain of clothing outlets to be responsive to the changing needs of their customers. The manager immediately understood the genius of what Penney was proposing: "What you are planning, sir, is an organization that will always be renewing itself from within!"

We now know Penney had the right idea: truly great business leaders create self-renewing organizations. And that's what Jim Penney achieved at what would become—for a brief period, at least—the world's leading retailer. Unfortunately, Penney lost interest in the business he founded before he had a chance to institutionalize the organizational capacities needed for the company to sustain the agility it would need to thrive in the long term. The J.C. Penney company is still around, of course. But for decades it has been desperately thrashing about, trying one me-too strategy after another in a constant struggle to keep afloat in the ever-changing world of retailing.

The history of J.C. Penney is, sadly, much like that of dozens of other formerly great companies ranging from General Motors to Motorola to Hewlett-Packard. In fact, most large companies seem doomed to a cycle of lurching from success to crisis, then frantically trying to regain their former excellence by way of large-scale, disruptive, costly—and typically ineffective—organizational change programs.

But there are exceptions to this general rule of unsustainable success—specifically, a small number of notable companies with long-term records of high performance (as measured in cold cash). And management consultants and professors (like me) have been trying (and failing) for decades to figure out how they accomplish this trick. But as the authors of this path-breaking book convincingly demonstrate, we have been barking up the wrong tree: there is no such trick to be found.

In fact, there is no magic formula, no secret sauce, no five, ten (or even twenty) "best practices" that lead to sustainable high performance. In hindsight, we should have been able to see that. After all, if great management consisted of simply adopting a universally effective set of policies or practices, all companies would follow suit and ape the actions of the leaders in their industries—*et voilà*, they'd all be equally as successful as the best. What we learn from *The Agility Factor* is that it ain't that easy. The long-term and repeated successes of high performers are actually due—in the main—to their hard, constant, and never-ending struggles to continually reinvent themselves.

The authors of this remarkable book—my former (full disclosure) colleagues Chris Worley, Tom Williams, and Ed Lawler—have spent the better part of the last eight years collecting and analyzing the data they present here in an admirably concise, useful, and readable form. Instead of asserting their findings, they *demonstrate them* with reference to their massive database of 60 companies and 4,700 directors and executives. In short, *they have the numbers*—and they use those logically and analytically to back up their findings. This is serious research, yet the result isn't sterile, impractical, academic theory. They clearly illustrate their findings with real-world examples of how high-performing companies continually recreate themselves. Step by step, the authors lead us through the dynamic processes, or "systems of integrated routines," that give companies the capacity to make the timely changes in their products, policies, practices, and strategies that result in besting their competitors in the marketplace, time and again.

Although what these agile companies do is neither simple nor easy to replicate, it appears learnable—given the proper will, dedication, and leadership. Let's face it, it isn't easy for even the best companies to always keep themselves open to change. After all, success has a subversive way of making people and organizations feel, well, a bit smug, self-satisfied, and, ultimately, complacent. In sum, today's success breeds tomorrow's failure. Unless, that is, the organization develops the habits of mind that lead them to be constantly self-critical; dissatisfied with their performance, no matter how stellar; enamored of change; and constantly vigilant for the telltale signs of complacency. Our authors show us what those rare organizational traits actually look like in the cultures of a few companies that not only see change as normal but have built the capacities that, paradoxically, make change routine. Those routines, mind you, are not *practices*; rather, they are integrated systems that amount to having a culture of continual improvement. Eventually those systems and routines get into the DNA of organizations, and they become so habitually focused on the future, so used to always adapting to new challenges and trying new things, and so accustomed to taking calculated risks, that they become unaware that they are doing so—and of how unusual their behavior is in the domain of large corporations. What makes all this so difficult is that acquiring those habits necessary for agility requires managers to forgo the comforts of the familiar and tried and true, and for leaders to set aside the ego-satisfying feeling of knowing it all. Hey, it's no fun having to do things differently all the time, having to always relearn and unlearn, having to be open to the unusual and the new, and, especially, having to listen to contrarians and heretics (and even a few "crazies")!

I leave it to the authors to tell you why they have adopted the cheetah as a symbol of the kind of organizations they are describing. I once spent a bit of time in Africa and actually had a few occasions to observe the behavior of wild cheetahs. The ones I saw were *always on the prowl*. These speedy, agile cats know that if they sit still for too long in any one place they will be devoured by the voracious lions, leopards, and hyenas who compete against them for the same game. Thus, as tempting as it might be after a successful hunt to establish a camp in which to stretch out for a long nap, cheetahs know that if they don't keep moving they will end up as some other beast's lunch. And so it is with companies. For example, during the years when Motorola was a high-flying tech superstar, its leaders often hummed the mantra of its founder, Paul Galvin; to whit, "Always be in motion!" But when a company has a (metaphorically speaking) full belly, the temptation is to kick back and have a satisfying little snooze. And that's a big part of what happened at such formerly great industry leaders as Motorola, GM, HP, U.S. Steel, RCA, and J.C. Penney: zzzzzzz.

But that doesn't have to happen to your company. Thanks to this useful little book, you can learn what capacities your organization needs to develop in order to *always be in motion*. And you will see how the hard work required for agility can pay off handsomely in the long term. And you can trust the authors' conclusions: *They've got the numbers.*

Santa Clara, California   —James O'Toole
May 2014   Senior Fellow
                        Markkula Center for Applied Ethics
                                Santa Clara University

PREFACE

Wherever we are, it is but a stage on the way to
somewhere else, and whatever we do, however well
we do it, it is only a preparation to do something
else that shall be different.

—ROBERT LOUIS STEVENSON

This book is about organization agility and its performance consequences. Despite the volume of writing on the subject, the business and
academic press rarely connect these two issues in any meaningful
and concrete way. There is a lot of discussion about agile software
development in the technology community; agile culture and leadership,
among management gurus and in the blogosphere; agile manufacturing
practices, among operations experts; agile supply chains, among logis-
tics professionals; and agile organizations, among executives and academics. But there is little in the way of a demonstrated connection
between any of these forms of agility and organization performance.
The connection between agility and performance is often implied but
rarely established.

Moreover, there is considerable debate over what "good performance" actually means. Does a high stock price today mean the
organization is performing well? If the stock price falls tomorrow, is it
suddenly not performing well? How long must an organization sustain
high levels of profitability or stock price to be called successful?

Over the past seven years, our research and experience with large
corporations has unearthed two key findings concerning agility and
organization performance:

1. In every industry, there are three long-term patterns of profit performance. Some firms have profitability that is consistently below
   industry average, a larger proportion of firms have profitability that
   thrashes below and above average, and a few firms consistently
   outperform the industry.

2. The best explanation for the outperformance pattern is a capability we call *agility*—a system of routines that allows a company to make repeated organization changes when necessary. These consistently high-performing companies do a better job of revising their strategy, perceiving and interpreting environmental trends and disruptions, testing potential responses, and implementing the most promising changes. Agility of this type cannot be developed overnight, and it is not likely to emerge by accident. An agile organization must be built on an integrated foundation of management practices that create an adaptable organization.

ORIGINS OF THE BOOK

The stories, data, and conclusions in the following pages are the result of a long-term collaboration—the integration of two streams of thought that came together about six years ago. One stream of thought originated at Booz & Company (now Strategy&, the former commercial part of Booz Allen Hamilton). While working there, Tom Williams and Steve Wheeler wondered what light research might shed on helping organizations transform more quickly and reliably. As management consultants, they typically dealt with organizations that were in trouble. They found their clients in one of four states, only one of which was desirable. Companies were (1) "behind the curve," hurtling toward a crisis that demanded a performance transformation; (2) facing inconsistent execution of change initiatives that were not delivering expected results; (3) coming out of a transformation exhausted and frustrated; or (4) anticipating the need for the next transformation to take performance to a higher level. Booz & Company's efforts to improve execution—guiding client top management to establish clear objectives, to design a sequence of campaigns, and to execute those campaigns under tight control—usually delivered results. However, they also believed that there was something missing and that more could be done to improve the success rate of campaigns and to institutionalize new capabilities.

The other stream of thought originated at the Center for Effective Organizations (CEO), a research center within the Marshall School of Business at the University of Southern California where Sue Mohrman, Ed Lawler, and Chris Worley were thinking about the state of practice and research related to organization change. At the time, most writing began with impressive statistics about the percentage of change efforts that failed to meet expectations despite a large base of empirical studies and years of interventions. There was a strong feeling among academics and practitioners that organization change was misunderstood, and the usual remedy was to call for better tools and intervention processes.

Ed and Chris asked a different question. What if the failure rate of organization change was the result not of bad change management practice, but of time-honored design principles and assumptions that produced organizations that valued stability? The result of their inquiry, the book *Built to Change*, represented a vision of what an organization might look like if it replaced the *stability = effectiveness* assumption with the assumption that *changing = effectiveness*.

Jim O'Toole, a research scientist at the Center for Effective Organizations and a longtime advisor to Booz & Company, saw the parallels between the two streams and orchestrated a meeting. As the groups explored their different models and frameworks, the overlapping concepts and interests became clear. A key insight emerged when the groups realized that if executives viewed campaign implementation and capability building as the same thing, the ability to change could be institutionalized. An agile organization would not engage in periodic transformations with campaigns that were seen—and usually resisted— as "not invented here" intrusions. The organization would see change as normal.

The insight became a purpose: to understand if there were organizations that possessed such a capability and if that capability delivered sustained results.

The purpose spawned three streams of work. In the initial stream, the team reviewed the literature on strategic change, adaptation, and evolution. CEO's O'Toole, Worley, and Lawler worked with Booz's Williams and Adrienne Crowther to describe what was known. The review suggested that change was indeed possible but problematic. A few well-documented, popular, and successful cases of large-scale transformations stood in the shadow of a much larger number of failures. Similarly, empirical articles consistently found a few key predictors of successful change but rarely found the same key predictors.

Clearly, something was missing. On the one hand, no single change theory seemed to work in all cases. A wide variety of successful and unsuccessful organization changes were going on, and the existing theories and frameworks were struggling to account for these activities. As a result, managers were left holding the bag. Their only option was to choose their favorite approach from among a set of inadequate theories. On the other hand, most studies focused on a single change and, at best, short-term performance improvements. The link between change and long-term performance was not established, and the only good data asserted a negative relationship: change was associated with an increasing risk of failure. These two observations drove the second and third streams of work.

The second stream inquired into the possibility of sustained performance. Using prior research as our jumping-off point, we looked at the long-term financial performance of large public companies. In the end, our sample included 424 firms in twenty-two industries over thirty-two years (1980–2012). The findings of this research were summarized earlier in this Preface and are reported in Chapter One. It shows that consistent, above-average profitability, although rare, is possible.

In the third stream, we wanted to understand whether the high-performing organizations possessed an agility capability that other firms did not. Toward that end, we developed an organization survey and interview protocol. Questions for the survey and interview were developed by Tom Williams and Adrienne Crowther from Booz & Company and Ed Lawler, Sue Mohrman, and Chris Worley from CEO.

In the end, the core of the survey consisted of fifty-one items. The items rated an organization's strategies, structures, systems, and culture on a five-point scale, where 1 = not at all and 5 = to a great extent. The fifty-one items rolled up into fourteen initial scales. Based on the interview data, the fourteen scales eventually were grouped into the four routines of agility: strategizing, perceiving, testing, and implementing. For the interested reader, the e-book *Assessing Organization Agility* describes the survey and interview questions in more detail. It also provides access to a short form of the survey as well as assessment guidelines.

Over the next five years, Chris led the effort to gather data from large public corporations in different industries as well as data from nonprofits, privately held companies, and other types of organizations. Rather than accepting a single survey response from a senior executive to represent the whole firm, our approach was to work closely with an organization. We typically collected surveys and/or interviews from a top management team, a sample of senior managers, or a sample from a function or business unit. The data were then fed back to the organization for discussion and action planning. This allowed us to gain a deeper understanding of the survey and interview findings and to understand whether the data represented the traditional way an organization operated or not.

The final data set included surveys from over 4,700 directors and executives from sixty companies about the way their organizations formulate strategy, design their structures and work processes, lead their people, change, and innovate. Thirty-four of these companies were large firms in our public company financial performance database. All three performance patterns were present. Our interview sample was somewhat smaller; it represented nineteen of the thirty-four firms in our financial database.

When we compared the survey data with the financial performance data, we saw a strong relationship between an organization's profitability patterns and its approach to management—specifically, the ways it anticipated and responded to events in the outside world, solved problems, and implemented change. When an organization possessed three or four agility routines working together as a system, it was able to sustain an above-average level of performance. Whenever markets and technologies changed rapidly and unpredictably, as they did in every industry over the thirty-two years we studied, the outperformers successfully applied these routines and the others did not.

Our conclusion: Agility does more than allow firms to adapt. It makes them adaptable and proactively nimble. In environments that change continuously, unpredictably, and at an increasing rate, organizations must be able to change repeatedly if they are to maintain their environmental "fit" and survive. They also need to be able to change quickly enough to stay ahead of the environmental forces that can signal tough times or even the firm's demise.

OUTLINE OF THE BOOK

Chapter One describes our research on large company performance in twenty-two industries, from 1980 to 2012, and explores alternative explanations for the patterns we found. Given the breadth and depth of change in every competitive environment over those thirty-two years, an "initial endowment" hypothesis of locked-in advantage fails to explain how the outperformers managed to consistently beat the industry average. Similarly, an "excellent company" hypothesis of sustainable competitive advantage based on superior management practices is found wanting. The best explanation is that outperforming firms were able to adapt to environmental changes better than their competitors.

Chapter Two describes the Agility Pyramid and the four routines that comprise the agile capability through the lens of a major transformation at DaVita, a Fortune 500 health care provider that operates over 1,800 kidney dialysis centers in the United States and beyond. DaVita methodically built agility on top of a solid foundation of vision and values, good management practices, and clinical care capabilities. Along the way, they metamorphosed the culture to one of inclusion, engagement, execution, and accountability. DaVita's performance since 2000 speaks for itself.

Chapter Three explores the first two agility routines, strategizing and perceiving, in more detail. Nokia—despite its recent stumbles and Microsoft's acquisition of its devices business—provides a good example of how these routines, separately and in combination, operate to deliver the potential for competitive advantage. Potential, however, is not realized until something is implemented.

Chapter Four describes the testing and implementing routines of agility. The ability to run low-cost experiments and clearly determine their success or failure separates good ideas from merely feasible ones and helps focus implementation resources. Implementing changes to strategy, organization structure, capabilities, or the asset base is one of the distinguishing characteristics of agile organizations. Most managers believe their company possesses this ability, although the hard evidence suggests otherwise.

In Chapter Five, we describe the process of transforming to an agile organization and provide multiple company examples. Cambia Health Solutions, the diversified Blue Cross Blue Shield insurer, has set about transforming their regulated business into an agile organization. Allstate Insurance—one of the country's largest property, casualty, and life insurance providers—adopted advanced change processes to transform their organization. Finally, when Rich Teerlink took over from Vaughan Beals as CEO at Harley-Davidson, Teerlink and his management team chose to build an organization that would adapt and endure because it took advantage of everyone's abilities and insights. Over the course of a decade, Teerlink and his team built a solid foundation of good management practices and differentiated capabilities on which to base agility.

The Afterword completes the book by stepping back from the research results and practical recommendations to explore two "So what?" issues. While agile organizations may enjoy sustained financial performance, there's nothing stopping them from pursuing other ends for good or ill. We explore two positive applications of organization agility, including how agility might be used to support a broader sense of sustainability and a renaissance in the field of organization development.

FINAL THOUGHTS

The cheetah on the cover is our symbol of agility. Conventional wisdom has it that a cheetah's formidable survival skills are the result of its speed, sometimes approaching sixty miles per hour. More recent research, employing tracking collars equipped with GPS, accelerometers, and gyroscopes, has demonstrated that the cheetah can accelerate, decelerate, and change direction faster than anything else on the African savannah.[1] It has evolved into the fastest mammal on land, and one of the most agile creatures on earth.

A variety of theories and schools of thought guided the development of our frameworks. Throughout the book, there are a number of sidebars that enumerate particular topics in greater detail. The sidebars provide what we hope is a useful synopsis of these theoretical schools of thought and some key publications for the interested reader. Readers can safely skip these without losing our main lines of argument.

This is not a long book; that is by design. But brevity should not be mistaken for simple or simplistic. Agility is a very high-order management capability that involves complex interactions and sound judgment. Very few large corporations exhibit agility. However, those that do consistently outperform their industry peers. Our research does not offer a quick fix or silver bullet, and business readers do not need another doorstop that tells them how to turn their company into El Dorado. The journey to establish good management is long and hard. Agility is several leagues beyond that. But for managers, customers, employees, and shareholders, the journey seems to be worth it.

THE AGILITY
FACTOR

CHAPTER

SEARCHING FOR SUSTAINED PERFORMANCE

The world breaks everyone…those that will not
break, it kills. It kills the very good and the very
gentle and the very brave impartially. If you are
none of these, you can be sure it will kill you
too but there will be no special hurry.

—ERNEST HEMINGWAY

The business environment is a merciless place. Before Microsoft, Apple, or Google, there was the Digital Equipment Corporation (DEC). Ken Olsen and Harlan Anderson incorporated DEC in Maynard, Massachusetts, in 1957, the same year that Hewlett-Packard went public. The investment community was so hostile toward computers that Georges Doriot, whose American Research and Development Corporation provided seed capital, suggested they change the originally proposed company name, "Digital Computer Corporation."

DEC created the minicomputer with its PDP (Programmable Data Processor) family of machines. These interactive computers became mainstays of research departments, engineering laboratories, and academic institutions. Because it sold through original equipment manufacturers (OEMs) as well as directly, DEC was not burdened with costly application software development and peripheral configuration. In 1970, the PDP-11, DEC's first 16-bit computer, firmly established itself as the market leader. Ironically, it was a crash program in response to Data General's NOVA machine, which had been developed by an engineering team of DEC defectors in 1968. Ultimately, over six hundred thousand PDP-11s of all models were sold. Most, if not all, of the computer engineers who created the PC revolution learned to program on PDP-11s.

In 1978, DEC introduced the 32-bit VAX (Virtual Address eXtension) computer, arguably the most successful minicomputer ever made. By 1990, VAX had propelled DEC to the number two position in the computer industry, behind IBM. That year, its peak, DEC had revenue of $14 billion and employed 120,000 people worldwide.

Eight years later, the Digital Equipment Corporation was gone, acquired by PC maker Compaq at a "discounted" price. In 1977, Ken Olsen had famously derided the emerging personal computer, saying, "There is no reason for any individual to have a computer in his home." Unfortunately for Olsen, it was the dream of Apple cofounder Steve Wozniak to have a PDP-11 in his home. Digital was late with personal computers, introducing three product lines that were incompatible with each other and with emerging industry standards. They stuck with proprietary architectures and operating systems while the industry moved toward standardization and interoperability. They were slow to adopt UNIX and provide customers with access to its extensive suite of application software.

DEC's product group organization structure went from strength to liability as competition among different subgroups squandered resources and missed market opportunities. Olsen reorganized DEC three times between 1988 and 1991 in increasingly desperate attempts to regain focus and competitiveness. The result was confusion and defection; some of the best and brightest at DEC are now elsewhere, running major technology organizations.

After posting eleven straight profitable years between 1980 and 1990, DEC lost money in five of its last seven years, and Olsen was removed by the board in 1995. When it was acquired by Compaq in 1998, DEC employed 53,500 people, half of its 1990 peak. Four years later, Compaq was acquired by Hewlett-Packard.

SURVIVING VERSUS THRIVING

Digital's spectacular rise and fall over a forty-year arc is unusual in the business world. We tend to think of corporations as long-lived entities that span many human generations. Companies such as Ford Motor, Harley-Davidson, DuPont, Siemens, or General Electric have celebrated over a century of existence. But while the experience of these companies is not unique, they are the exceptions, not the rule. Most start-up companies—in fact, most organizations—do not last very long. Recent research suggests that the expected life of a new American company is on the order of six years.[1] DEC lasted forty years, although the company that bought it, Compaq, had a total life span of only twenty years. Corporate life, like human life, can be nasty, brutish, and short. As Exhibit 1.1 shows, over the past forty years, about half of the U.S. Fortune 500 fell off the list each decade as companies dissolved, were acquired, or underwent a change of control and ceased to exist as independent going concerns.

EXHIBIT 1.1. *Survival Rates of Fortune 500 Firms*

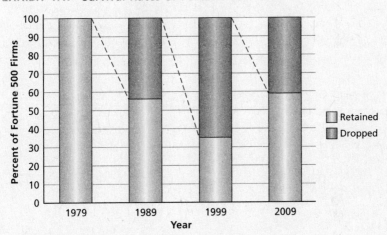

The Old Way of Defining Sustained Performance

Survival is hard enough, but most people—investors and managers in particular—are interested in financial performance. The goal of "maximizing shareholder returns" is usually held up as the primary objective of management. Total shareholder return (TSR) is the preferred performance metric and, in the United States, the S&P 500 stock index is the appropriate benchmark for "the market" (see "Shareholder Returns" sidebar). These financial market measures are "objective," are difficult to manipulate over anything but the very short term, reflect outside investors' perceptions of value, and have the benefit of being a single measure against which *any* public firm can be judged.

The data suggest that maximizing shareholder value over the long run is as hard as surviving. No company, for example, has consistently beaten "the market." As Foster and Kaplan wrote in 2001:

...long-term studies of corporate birth, survival, and death in America clearly show that the corporate equivalent of El Dorado, the golden company that continually performs better than the markets, *has never existed*. It is a myth. Managing for survival, even among the best and most revered corporations, does not guarantee strong long-term performance for shareholders. In fact, just the opposite is true. In the long run, markets always win.[2]

Equity markets are subject to fads, irrational exuberance, and panics that have little to do with the quality of the business strategy, management insight, and organization designs that produce profits. Although all industries are subject to the effects of recession, inflation, and social change, the relative performance of industries changes according to their own events and cycles, causing even industry darlings to revert to market means. As a result, stock price and the resultant calculation of shareholder return are inadequate measures of both management effectiveness and sustained performance.[3]

SHAREHOLDER RETURNS

Finance theory holds that stock prices represent the market's rational expectations for future performance, and shareholder returns are a popular metric for determining absolute or relative performance for publicly traded companies. The rate of total shareholder returns (TSR) for any given time period is calculated as:

$$TSR = ((P_E - P_B + D)/P_B) - 1$$

Where:

P_E is the price per share at the end of the period;

P_B is the price per share at the beginning of the period; and

D is dividends per share paid in the period.

For example, Exhibit 1.2 shows monthly TSR, in percent, for ExxonMobil from May 1997 to June 2002. These returns swing from a high of 17.7 percent to a low of −8.6 percent.

Plotting cumulative TSR provides a way to "see" what is happening to the value of an investment over time. By convention, the plot starts with a value of 1, as in $1 worth of ExxonMobil, and compounds intraperiod returns to create a graphical view of investment growth or decline. Cumulative TSR (CTSR) is given by the formula:

$$CTSR_t = CTSR_{t-1} * (1 + TSR_t)$$

EXHIBIT 1.2. *ExxonMobil Monthly Total Shareholder Returns*

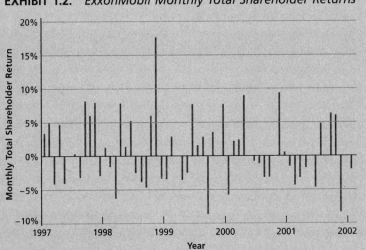

Where:

CTSR$_t$ is the cumulative TSR in time period t;

CTSR$_{t-1}$ is the cumulative TSR in time period t − 1 (the prior period); and

TSR$_t$ is the total shareholder return in time period t (as calculated above). The monthly cumulative TSR for ExxonMobil from May 1997 to June 2002 is shown in Exhibit 1.3.

At the end of our example five-year period, in June 2002, the index value is 1.48. That is, the value of our $1 investment in Exxon has grown to $1.48 of ExxonMobil, with a lot of ups and downs in between. Notice that if we calculated the simple TSR from May 16, 1997, to June 2, 2002, it would be the same 48 percent. Given the volatility of share prices and shareholder returns, TSR and CTSR are very sensitive to start dates and end dates.

The reason for starting on May 16, 1997, is that was the date of Amazon's initial public offering. The cumulative TSR for Amazon stock is shown in Exhibit 1.4.

Amazon took shareholders on a wild ride, to a high of fifty-seven times their initial investment in February 1999 before settling at a little over ten times in June 2002. The TSR for Amazon between May 1997 and

(Continued)

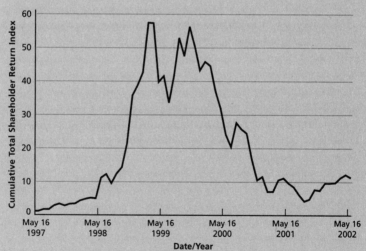

EXHIBIT 1.3. *ExxonMobil Cumulative Total Shareholder Returns*

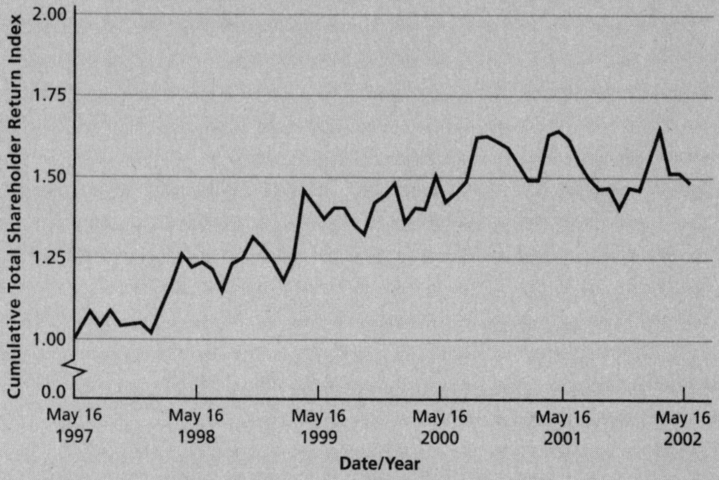

EXHIBIT 1.4. *Amazon Cumulative Total Shareholder Returns*

EXHIBIT 1.5. *Cumulative Total Shareholder Returns Comparison*

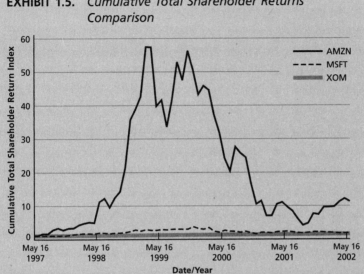

June 2002 was 1,023 pecent, but that calculation would not reveal what happened between those dates.

A comparison of cumulative TSRs was used in *Good to Great* and *What Really Works* to distinguish "high performing" companies from the rest.[4] Exhibit 1.5 compares cumulative TSR for Amazon, ExxonMobil, and Microsoft from May 1997 to June 2002.

As can be seen, ExxonMobil and Microsoft barely register when compared to Amazon. So which is the high performing company? That depends entirely on your perspective. Is performance absolute or relative? Is it a function of stock price or economic value (that is, profit) created?

Over this period, ExxonMobil had annual ROAs of between 5.5 percent and 11.9 percent, and beat its average industry ROA every year. Amazon did not report its first quarterly profit until January 2002. Amazon's share price benefited from the dot-com bubble, during which investors were assured that the economic logic of profitability no longer applied. Exxon's share price reflected a depressed industry that led to a new round of consolidation, during which Exxon acquired Mobil. While you might have preferred to own Amazon stock over this period, ExxonMobil was the clear outperformer in terms of economic value delivered.

A valid alternative to shareholder returns as a measure of comparative performance is accounting profitability, calculated as return on assets or return on equity. Managers, as opposed to shareholders, invest in their businesses and look to survive, compete, and grow *within their industry*. The robust business of industry benchmarking and best practices attests to managers' desire to know how they are doing relative to peers as well as what peers are doing differently to deliver superior or inferior returns. What matters is relative performance in their own environment. The jaguar does not care what happens on the African savannah but is very concerned with what happens in the Brazilian rain forests.

Anita McGahan, in an important and often overlooked series of articles, mined Compustat's "business segment" (operating units or divisions of corporations) database for the period 1981–1997 looking for patterns of performance to help guide expectations for managers and researchers.[5] She screened 13,574 reporting entities—groups of similar operating units or business segments—with annual sales or assets of at least $10 million within 8,018 U.S. corporations in 664 industries. The study ranked business segments according to accounting profitability (the ratio of operating income to assignable assets, or ROA) in the first four years the segment appeared (but mostly 1981–1984, as most firms were present for the entire period) and the last four years the segment appeared (but mostly between 1993–1997). McGahan defined sustained high performance as being in the top quartile of profitability in the first four years and the last four years of the time series. Her results are shown in Exhibit 1.6.

EXHIBIT 1.6.   *McGahan's Performance Data*

	Final Performance Position		
Initial Performance Position	**Top Quartile**	**Middle**	**Bottom Quartile**
Top Quartile	Sustained High Performance (19.4%)		Declining Performers (9.8%)
Middle		Steady Moderate Performance (40.7%)	
Bottom Quartile	Rising Performers (10.5%)		Chronic Underperformance (19.6%)

Source: Adapted from McGahan, 1999, Figure 4.

What surprised McGahan, and us too, was the persistence of the relative rankings. Looking at the diagonal cells from upper left to lower right, we see that 79.7 percent of the firms that began the period as a top, medium, or bottom performer ended the period in the same category. Only 10.5 percent of the firms (the lower-left three cells) were able to move up in performance, and of those only 0.5 percent were able to make the jump (over a sixteen-year period) from bottom to top. When the measure of performance was profitability and the benchmark was an arbitrary but reasonable 25th percentile of performance for all firms, there was a clear pattern of sustained performance.

Despite these real insights, McGahan's conclusions are vulnerable to several challenges. First, looking at only the first four and last four years of a period ignores the time in between (almost ten years) in which important events may have affected the pattern of performance. Performance could have varied up or down within those four-year periods as well as in the interim. A firm that is a high performer at the beginning and end but performs poorly in between does not deserve to be called a sustained high performer. Such a pattern suggests a very different performance dynamic. Second, McGahan's definition of "industry" used the old Standard Industrial Classification (SIC) system. As a result, some categories, as she noted, lumped very different businesses together (for example, pharmaceutical companies and agricultural firms). Explaining performance variation with such a broad definition of industry may be washing out some pure industry effects.

These concerns prompted us to ask three additional questions:

- What happens if you look at a more continuous picture of performance over a longer time period?

- What does this picture look like using a finer-grained view of industry (read "environment")?

- What are the implications for CEOs and their top management teams?

A Different Way of Defining Sustained Performance

To answer the first two questions, we went back to the Compustat database and analyzed annual ROA (annual net income/total assets) and annual TSR (annual share price returns adjusted for dividends and stock splits) data from 1980 to 2012—about twice as long as McGahan's time frame and inclusive of the Great Recession of 2008–2009. Instead of the segment database McGahan examined, we used the annual database to get a more continuous view of the performance for whole organizations, although we deliberately excluded diversified firms such as General Electric, Ingersoll-Rand, Emerson, Eaton, Berkshire Hathaway, and United Technologies. We used three benchmarks: the annual S&P 500 stock index rate of return, annual industry mean TSR, and annual industry mean ROA for the firms in our sample. We were guided by the ICB classification for industry rather than SIC or NAICS. The ICB system often breaks up a North American Industry Classification System (NAICS) category into competitive peer groups with more "face validity" and provides a better proxy for environment. Our data set comprised 424 companies in 22 industries.[6]

We defined "sustained organization performance" from a management perspective: winning in a particular environment. Specifically, if an organization posted annual ROA or TSR above a particular benchmark at least 80 percent of the time (26.5 out of 32 years), it demonstrated sustained performance.

As expected, when the measure was TSR, only one firm was able to beat "the market" more than 80 percent of the time (Holiday Corporation, in eight out of ten years for which data were available). Out of the 424 firms in our sample, only thirty were able to beat the 70-percent mark. Even fewer firms—as in none—were able to beat the 80-percent standard when the benchmark was industry average shareholder return (only eight firms beat the industry average TSR more than 70 percent of the time). Apparently, it's even harder to beat your peers than it is to beat the market!

When the benchmark measure of performance was average industry ROA, we anticipated finding patterns similar to McGahan's (and we did), but we were surprised by their nature and persistence. In every industry we analyzed over this thirty-two-year period, we observed three patterns of performance:

- Firms that outperformed the industry mean ROA at least 80 percent of the time (18 percent of the sample)

- Firms that underperformed the industry mean at least 80 percent of the time (13 percent of the sample)

- Firms that "thrashed" between periods of underperformance and outperformance relative to the industry mean (68 percent of the sample)

Unlike shareholder returns against the market, relative performance against industry profitability can be long-lived. As with McGahan's results, outperformers tend to remain outperformers and underperformers remain underperformers. However, unlike McGahan's "steady moderate" group, the middle 50 percent of her distribution, our "thrashers" label is more descriptive of the performance pattern. Thrashers remained thrashers, suggesting considerable inconsistency rather than mere mediocrity. Also in line with McGahan's data, across all the industries we studied, we found only three firms—Harley-Davidson, IBM, and DaVita—that "broke out" of their thrasher or underperformer pattern and changed to achieve consistently high performance for the remainder of the period.

Chapter Appendix One displays these different pictures of performance for several of the industries we studied. But they all tell the same story. A managerial view of performance suggests that a few organizations can and do consistently outperform industry profitability, rather than attempting to beat a market rate of return. But more important, for a majority of firms life is a series of ups and downs, a dizzying pattern of boom and bust in which success and failure are just as easily ascribed to whoever is sitting in the captain's chair (whether or not they had anything to do with it) as to any organizational strategy or capability. Thrashers make for good stories as they cycle between damnation and redemption at the hands of scapegoat or hero CEOs.

THE AGILITY FACTOR

What accounts for sustained performance? Management and organization theory holds that successful firms have a high degree of fit or alignment with their environments. The products and services offered and the way they are delivered respond to the demands of the environment, and management has many choices as to how to make this happen. One way is to just muddle through—what researchers call "ad hoc problem solving." This form of adapting is intentional and rational, not merely reactive or passive, and does not depend on repetitive behavior.[7] When a problem presents itself, organization members engage in a search for solutions. This behavior has been researched extensively; it was first described by the economist Herbert Simon in 1947.[8] The research shows that since a thorough and exhaustive search under time pressure is unlikely, managers will "satisfice" rather than optimize. They will often take the first solution that appears to have any chance of solving the problem. As a result, luck is just as likely as ad hoc problem solving to explain a pattern of sustained performance. Admonishing managers to "be lucky" is neither insightful nor useful, although Napoleon had the right idea when he said, "I don't want generals who are brilliant. I want generals who are lucky."

More systematically, practitioners and researchers have developed three broad perspectives to explain how and why organizations could maintain this alignment between their organizations and the environment. These perspectives can be called the Darwinian selection argument, the organization physics argument, and the dynamic capabilities argument.

Darwinian Selection Argument

The first explanation is best framed by the population ecology school of business research.[9] Researchers adopting this perspective have constructed and analyzed rich data sets that have led to a wealth of insight regarding a merciless Darwinian world where, industry by industry, organization change is accomplished by the birth of new organization forms and the death of old organizations that are incapable of changing.

In the standard telling of industrial evolution, large, established, inert firms are overtaken by small, upstart, nimble ones that grow to look and behave like their victims, and the cycle repeats. The forces at work are the same as those in biological ecosystems: variation, selection, and retention. This is the basic argument advanced by Clayton Christensen in *The Innovator's Dilemma*.[10] DEC was unable to see the value of the emerging, disruptive PC technology and, despite great effort, was unable to adapt in time.

Sadly, this school of thought offers little solace to managers of companies that find themselves in trouble. Organization inertia—the inability to change at a rate at least equal to environmental change—is the result of commitments to courses of action that constrain responses. As organizations grow in size and the longer they live, the more inert and resistant to change they become. When the forces of "natural selection" come calling, they are so overwhelming that attempts to change a company to realign its fit with the environment have very low probabilities of success.

Turning this logic on its head, if environments are stable, inertia would be a strength; that is, an organization could sustain high levels of performance if it possessed an initial advantage at the beginning of a time period. For example, one might argue that Microsoft's admirable profitability record is a function of its early dominance in PC operating systems. Despite tremendous changes in the software industry, one thing has remained amazingly stable since Microsoft's inception: people have been buying lots of computers with Windows, and that initial advantage has paid off handsomely in profits. This might also explain Apple's current domination in mobile devices or eBay's in online auctions.

Some industries have a "winner take all" dynamic that means an initial advantage and superior position can be sustained if certain core parts of the environment remain stable, particularly if network effects amplify a product's value. This argument does not, however, represent a very good general explanation for the performance patterns we see.

In particular, there is little support for the conclusion that environments are stable and organization inertia is a competitive advantage. For example, it was not obvious at the beginning that Microsoft or Apple or Amazon would win in the industry shakeout. CPM and UNIX were technically superior operating systems, Motorola and Nokia had dominant positions in mobile phones, and Peapod, J.C. Penney, and Yahoo were on the Internet well before Amazon. It is pretty hard to argue that these environments were "stable."

In fact, recent research has found that market environments have become increasingly turbulent over the past decade, and that the persistence of competitive advantage and sustained performance has gotten shorter.[11] "Hypercompetition," D'Aveni's term for when competitive conditions are so turbulent and uncertain that the competitive advantages and profits resulting from them cannot be sustained, has become a reality in almost every industry.[12] Over the thirty-two years covered in our database, there has been tremendous change in the political, technical, and economic landscape as well as significant increases in the breadth and depth of global competition.

In 1980, it was "morning in America," and Paul Volcker was about to unleash the first of four recessions in the period. The Soviet Union was intact, albeit on life support. China was a closed economy, India a socialist country with significant Soviet trade. Japan was ascendant, and the Asian Tigers were cubs. GM had over 40 percent of U.S. light vehicle market share. The IBM antitrust investigation had dragged on for eleven years. Utilities markets in the United States and Europe were highly regulated. The era of investor capitalism and the corporate raider was just beginning. There were no cell phones, Internet, or satellite navigation systems, and few personal computers. There was no WTO; the GATT Uruguay Round would not take place until 1986. Moreover, between 1980 and 2012, mergers, breakups, spin-offs, alliances, new entrants, and changing boundaries have altered the face of most industries.

Within-industry change has been equally mind numbing. For example, the oil and gas industry has experienced dramatic technological changes in exploration, refining, and transportation. In 1980, there were no "mini-marts" on every corner, little shale gas, no horizontal drilling, no deep-water exploration, and no 3-D seismic tools. Natural gas markets have been deregulated, federal taxes on gasoline in the

United States have increased 325 percent, and environmental regulation in response to industry incidents has proliferated. Still, outperformers have adapted and maintained or enhanced their environmental fit. ExxonMobil's performance was industry leading when oil was $8 bbl. *and* when it was $147 bbl.

Consequently, there is no empirical support for the notion that an advantaged set of initial endowments and stable environments explain the persistence of the outperforming companies we found.

Organizational Physics Argument

The second explanation is framed by the "excellent company" research. Store shelves groan under the weight of best-selling books purporting to explain how companies can become good, excellent, great, or visionary. These "secrets of business success" may be simple or complex, but, like exercise programs or diets, they all hold out the promise of results by applying the laws of organizational physics: *Do these things, and improved performance will surely follow.* In contrast to the suggestion that organizations cannot change, the excellent company perspective says that managers have considerable sway or "strategic choice" over organizational operations and can chart strategies and courses of action to achieve high performance despite environmental change. This perspective rejects the claim that organizations cannot change; instead, it proposes that there is a "right" way to manage.

Peters and Waterman proposed one of the initial formulas for success in their classic *In Search of Excellence*, which contained much praise for Digital Equipment Corporation.[13] They proposed eight organizational prescriptions, including a bias for action, stick to the knitting, stay close to the customer, simultaneous loose-tight properties, productivity through people, simple form and lean staff, and so on. Similarly, Jim Collins articulated a number of organizational habits to cultivate and deadly sins to avoid in *Built to Last* and *Good to Great*.[14] In *Good to Great*, for example, he claimed to provide "timeless, universal answers that can be applied by any organization" (p. 5). If the organizational physics argument held, then these firms should consistently demonstrate our definition of sustained performance.

Exhibit 1.7 shows the number of years that total shareholder return has been above the S&P 500 stock index from 1980 to 2012 for the *Built to Last* and *Good to Great* companies. Even though both studies used similar techniques—cumulative shareholder returns—only Philip Morris, the tobacco company, showed up on both lists. On a year-over-year basis, seventeen out of twenty-three firms were able to beat the market more than 50 percent of the time; the two best,

EXHIBIT 1.7. *Market Performance of* Good to Great *and* Built to Last *Companies Between 1980 and 2012*

Built to Last Companies*	Years of TSR/ROA Data 1980–2012	Years/ Percentage Above S&P 500	Years/ Percentage Above Industry TSR	Years/ Percentage Above Industry Average Profitability
American Express	33/33	22 (69%)	17 (53%)	19 (59%)
Boeing	33/33	22 (69%)	19 (59%)	10 (31%)
Citicorp	25/32	16 (60%)	12 (48%)	8 (25%)
Ford	33/33	14 (44%)	17 (53%)	11 (34%)
Hewlett-Packard	33/33	18 (56%)	11 (34%)	21 (66%)
IBM	33/33	15 (47%)	16 (50%)	21 (66%)
Johnson & Johnson	33/33	17 (53%)	17 (53%)	30 (94%)
Marriott	14/20	10 (71%)	5 (36%)	18 (90%)
Merck	33/33	20 (63%)	13 (41%)	25 (78%)
Motorola	33/33	16 (50%)	13 (41%)	16 (50%)
Nordstrom	33/33	20 (63%)	16 (50%)	7 (22%)
Procter & Gamble	33/33	19 (59%)	16 (50%)	13 (41%)
Sony	33/33	15 (47%)	13 (41%)	8 (25%)
Wal-Mart	33/33	19 (59%)	21 (66%)	32 (100%)
Walt Disney	33/33	20 (61%)	17 (52%)	31 (94%)
Good to Great Companies*				
Abbott Laboratories	33/33	18 (56%)	18 (56%)	24 (75%)
Circuit City	31/28	17 (55%)	14 (45%)	12 (43%)
Kimberly-Clark	33/33	21 (66%)	14 (44%)	11 (34%)
Kroger	33/33	20 (63%)	18 (56%)	15 (47%)
Nucor	33/33	19 (58%)	17 (52%)	32 (97%)
Pitney Bowes	33/33	15 (47%)	15 (47%)	7 (22%)
Walgreens	33/33	17 (53%)	20 (63%)	19 (59%)
Wells Fargo	33/33	19 (59%)	19 (59%)	7 (22%)

*General Electric, Philip Morris, Gillette, Fannie Mae, and 3M were deleted from the lists because they either were acquired, were too diversified, or lacked publicly available data for this study.
Note: The results are essentially the same when the median is used instead of the mean for industry comparisons.

Kimberly-Clark and Boeing, beat it 66 percent and 69 percent of the time, respectively. However, over the long haul they all faltered. When we apply the managerial perspective of performance within industry, only four of these organizations were able to meet the 80-percent standard with respect to ROA: Johnson & Johnson (94 percent), Nucor (96 percent), Walt Disney (94 percent), and Wal-Mart (100 percent).

Proponents of the organizational physics argument have responded to these criticisms. They note, accurately, that even excellent or visionary or great companies are bound to stumble. The response is fair but misses the point. The issue is not whether the principles are right, but whether these firms truly belong in the club of the well managed. Merely asking consultants or other CEOs who the best companies are does not specify the criteria for inclusion, whereas measures of cumulative shareholder return suffer from the weaknesses noted earlier. As one set of critics claimed, "It is startling to us that some of the great companies would not have been classified as such if their performance results were tabulated starting a few months differently from the starting month selected."[15]

Investors are deeply concerned about today's shareholder value but also about how that value accumulates over time. But managers and management researchers want to know if the organization knows what it is doing, and shareholder returns, by themselves, tell them little about the robustness of an organization's strategy or capability. Thus we part ways with these authors when it comes to their proposition that these companies were well managed, sustained high performers and their methods should be emulated. When the measure of performance was cumulative shareholder return, the relationship, according to data developed by others as well as our own, was not supported.

Dynamic Capabilities Argument

The third explanation is best framed by the "dynamic capabilities" school.[16] In contrast to the assumption of organization inertia in population ecology or a management formula in the organization physics perspective, this argument suggests that consistently high performers possess a capability to change their resources and processes repeatedly; they have the strategies, structures, resources, processes, and routines that allow them to both sense and adapt to environmental threats and opportunities as well as intentionally execute on strategic initiatives. These dynamic capabilities deliver appropriate organization changes when and where they are needed.[17] Rather than adhere to a particular set of management practices expected to serve them well under any and all circumstances, firms with healthy dynamic capabilities build (and drop) a variety of "normal" capabilities, possess organization structures that adjust, and so on. Sometimes they "stick to the knitting" and sometimes they diversify a little; sometimes they get really close to their customers and sometimes they distance themselves; sometimes they use "homegrown" management and sometimes they bring in outsiders; sometimes they use Level 5 leadership and sometimes a new direction will be dictated; and sometimes good enough is good enough.

Absent a dynamic capability that supports continuous change, organizations often adopt a "punctuated equilibrium" perspective on change.[18] This model suggests that organization change and performance follow similar patterns. Over relatively long periods of time, organizations converge on a particular solution and organization design that yields high levels of performance. When the environment changes, the organization's existing offerings and operations become misaligned with the new demands. Performance drops, quickly or slowly, and eventually forces the organization into transformation—a relatively short period of discontinuous organization change. In response to these compelling opportunities or violent shifts, firms often adopt reactive change management practices that set new objectives and develop new practices intended to move the organization from its current state to a future one that will, it is hoped, be more aligned with environmental demands. Research and experience suggest that when these transformations are conducted quickly and effectively, often with the help of outside consultants, they ensure survival and set the organization on another steady path of low organization change. However, research also suggests that only one third of these transformations deliver their anticipated results.

In the face of continued marketplace shifts and new challenges to performance, leadership reluctantly realizes that they have to go through the whole process again. Weary, battered, and bruised from the prior effort, the organization finds itself facing transformation after transformation and ends up with "change fatigue." This seems to describe well what happened at DEC as they reorganized three times in three years before ultimately being acquired.

Firms with a strong set of dynamic capabilities would manifest a performance pattern consistent with our outperformers, whereas firms without dynamic capabilities and following a punctuated equilibrium approach to change would manifest a thrasher pattern—high levels of performance for a time followed by low levels of performance. The relative duration of high or low performance would depend on the organization's ability to conduct timely and effective transformations.

In every industry we studied, there was at least one firm that was able to post consistently above-average performance over a thirty-plus-year period. Campbell's Soup in food and beverage; GlaxoSmithKline in pharmaceuticals; Johnson & Johnson in consumer products; Emerson Electric in electronics; Gap, Inc., in apparel; and Walgreens in drugstore retail have all posted consistently high levels of performance. Do these firms—many of which are not the ones we hear about in the business press—possess some unique capability that allows them to consistently outperform their peers?

In contrast, the thrashers—including BP, Procter & Gamble, IBM, Toyota, Pfizer, and Apple—are generally highly regarded companies that have received spectacular press at times but also tend to be admired for their peaks and forgiven for their valleys. They all have a pattern of breaking out of periods of underperformance, often through major transformations, only to fall back more than once over the thirty-year period. Each transformation was a high-risk, one-time occurrence that often started or ended with a CEO transition, technological change, or other key event. Although many business studies often support improved performance following well-executed transformations, there are no data regarding the sustainability of that performance. Instead, the organizations may have emerged exhausted rather than energized, complacent rather than paranoid. Critical changes and routines were not implemented well enough to affect performance, capabilities were not embedded, inertia was triumphant, and the cycle repeated.

CONCLUSION

Some large firms display a pattern of superior performance over long periods of time. A stable industrial environment does not explain these performance patterns. Since 1980, all industries have been subject to technological change, restructuring, regulatory change, and increasing global competition. These patterns are also not explained by the recommendations of "organizational physics." Example companies from *Built to Last, Good to Great*, and other studies are not consistent, long-term winners in their industries except by virtue of manipulated, investor-oriented, cumulative measures of performance.

Our data point to the conclusion that organizations with high levels of sustained performance have a capability to continuously adapt to their environments, see and exploit opportunities before others, and address threats quickly. This contrasts sharply with the change dynamic likely employed by the thrashers that launch transformations or other major change initiatives to temporarily achieve higher levels of performance, only to fall back in a few years. Such a capability would represent the important "something" that distinguishes outperformers from thrashers. The balance of our research aimed to understand and define that capability.

Superior performance is possible only when there is a high degree of fit between the requirements of the environment and the capabilities of the firm. In increasingly turbulent environments, this fit is temporary at best. *Agility* is the dynamic capability that allows outperforming firms to sense and respond to their environments and to rapidly reallocate resources, build new capabilities, and, perhaps most important, jettison the assets and activities that no longer create value. In a world where organizations are pressured to be predictable and reliable, these organizations have found a way to change and perform.

What we call the agility factor is an integrated set of routines that explains the difference between sustained high performance and boom/ bust cycles or sustained low performance. Agility is a dynamic capability that allows an organization to make timely, effective, and sustained responses to environmental change. It is more than "good management" and more than a single set of differentiating capabilities. Agility allows the organization to adapt, over and over again, in meaningful ways to support above-average performance over long periods of time.

CHAPTER ONE
APPENDIX

Exhibits 1.8 through 1.12 display several different pictures of sustained performance. For demonstration purposes, these figures display one or two sustained performers and selected thrashers or chronic underperformers.

Exhibit 1.8 graphs the ROA data for the oil and gas industry. ExxonMobil outperforms the industry average for twenty-nine of the thirty years (97 percent) and Royal Dutch Shell posted above-average returns 95 percent of the time. ExxonMobil exceeded the standard despite significant and well-publicized environmental, safety, and international missteps. On the other hand, BP—which was also in the news over the period as an equity market darling, sustainability leader, and environmental criminal—exceeded the industry average only eight of the thirty years (27 percent). ConocoPhillips is a classic thrasher, outperforming the average 43 percent of the time and showing a steep performance drop from 2005 to 2008.

Exhibit 1.9 depicts ROA performance for the automotive industry. The underperformance of GM and Ford's all-too-brief moments of profitability are clearly visible; GM beat the industry average only seven of twenty-eight years before filing for bankruptcy protection in 2008. Ford beat the industry average in eight of the thirty years. Over the same period, Toyota, which received many business press column inches for its Toyota Production System, Toyota Management System, and market share objectives of "global 10" and "global 15" only beat the average 75 percent of the time, while Honda quietly beat the average in twenty-seven of the years (90 percent). Nissan and Audi display the thrasher pattern.

Exhibit 1.10 shows ROA performance for selected pharmaceutical companies. Partially reflecting all of the press awarded to Merck as a "good to great" company, it exceeded the industry average ROA 73 percent of the time. Bristol-Myers Squibb exceeded the average 80 percent of the time, and GlaxoSmithKline beat the standard 77 percent of the time. Pfizer is a consistent underperformer that transformed into a thrasher around 1994, and Eli Lilly shows a similar pattern.

Exhibit 1.11 shows the ROA performance patterns for the retail apparel industry. Gap, Inc., despite its mercurial stock price performance, beats the industry average 83 percent of the time. Both Nike and Limited Brands consistently performed at or above the industry average 80 percent of the time. Although Nordstrom has a strong reputation, its profitability exceeded the industry average only 23 percent of the time. The industry thrashers, Levi Strauss and TJX Companies, have seen their profitability waver above and slightly below average for most of the period, achieving above-average performance 45 percent and 50 percent of the time, respectively.

Exhibit 1.12 presents the ROA performance of firms in the computer and office products industry. Xerox has consistently underperformed in the industry, while Dell and Lexmark have solid records of above-average performance. For all the attention they get, the thrashers in this industry are IBM and Apple, neither of which has been able to sustain above-average performance.

EXHIBIT 1.8.   *Oil and Gas Industry ROA Performance*

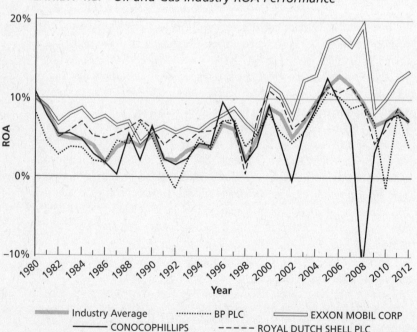

EXHIBIT 1.9. *Automobile Industry ROA Performance*

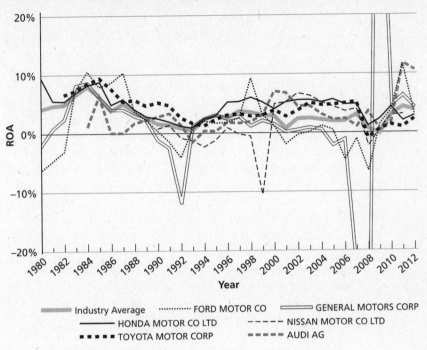

EXHIBIT 1.10. *Pharmaceutical Industry ROA Performance*

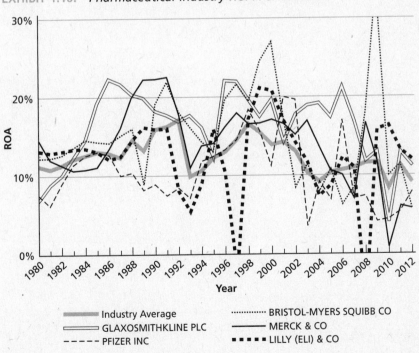

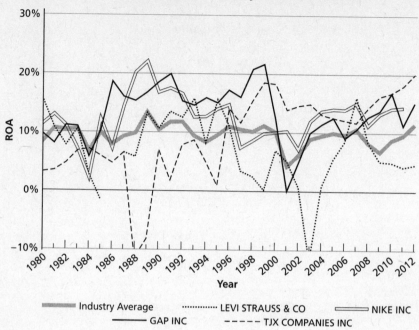

EXHIBIT 1.11. *Retail Apparel Industry ROA Performance*

Legend:
- Industry Average
- LEVI STRAUSS & CO
- NIKE INC
- GAP INC
- TJX COMPANIES INC

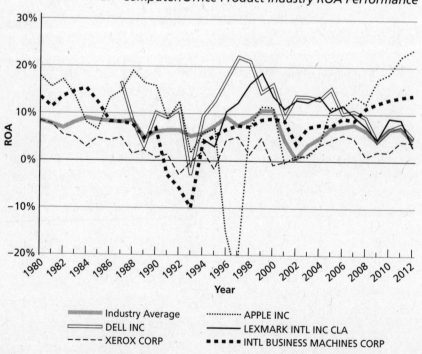

EXHIBIT 1.12. *Computer/Office Product Industry ROA Performance*

Legend:
- Industry Average
- APPLE INC
- DELL INC
- LEXMARK INTL INC CLA
- XEROX CORP
- INTL BUSINESS MACHINES CORP

CHAPTER

2

ORGANIZING
FOR AGILITY

Things alter for the worse spontaneously, if they
be not altered for the better designedly.

—FRANCIS BACON

Rande Somma, vice president of marketing at the Automotive Systems Group of Johnson Controls (JCI), knew he had to do something different if he was going to deliver on their chosen strategy of being a "solution provider" to the automotive OEMs. Until that point, JCI had successfully ridden the wave of automotive outsourcing by winning orders for car seats, manufacturing them, and delivering them just in time to assembly plants. However, they had little say in the design and engineering of the "seating systems," and they were at the mercy of their automotive customers when it came to managing the economics of the products JCI produced. JCI had little ability to challenge engineering designs demanded by the OEMs and absolutely no basis on which to dispute car-buyer requirements for seats, armrests, headrests, center consoles, cup holders, or any of the increasingly complex mechanisms that had made their way into automotive seating. To implement the solution provider strategy, JCI had to assume more control over the customer specification, design, and engineering of the car seats it produced.

So Rande decided to run an experiment on a Ford program that JCI had recently won. He contracted with a market research firm that the OEMs used to run several focus groups of JCI employees. They gathered their preferences among a set of design alternatives for seat systems in a minivan. The results were brought to the early-phase design meeting with the Ford team.

The initial response was not promising. The Ford team sat in stony silence as the JCI team presented findings that challenged a number of Ford's design requirements. However, the JCI team noted that Ford lacked any evidence-based rebuttal. Thus began a long process of presenting market research findings and counter-findings between the two teams. As JCI won a few skirmishes, they gained confidence as well as credibility with the Ford team and were able to improve their margins. Rande gradually diffused this capability to the GM and Chrysler customer teams at JCI.

One year later, end-customer market research was standard practice in every seat system development project. As a result, JCI was able to exercise much more control over seat system design and engineering and program economics. It also enabled JCI to become much more innovative and bring new ideas to their OEM customers. In one instance, JCI formed a relationship with Legos to make the toy an integral part of a minivan seating configuration.

The JCI story reflects lessons germane to an understanding of organization agility. It is clear from the case that Rande had a pretty deep knowledge of JCI's strategy and what it implied. His close relationship with the automobile customer gave him insight into how that strategy could be applied, and he had the autonomy and authority to try out ideas that he thought would work. Perhaps most important, JCI demonstrated the ability to put the changes in place and spread the innovation to other programs. Being able to repeatedly execute the process—from knowing the strategy, to perceiving a need, to running an experiment, to implementing a change that creates an advantage—is what distinguishes companies that outperform their competitors from the ones that do not.

ORGANIZATION AGILITY DEFINED

Agility is the capability to make timely, effective, and sustained organization changes. As with any capability, agility is a repeatable, organizational resource. Agile organizations are able to make *timely* changes because they can sense or anticipate relevant environmental shifts better than their peers. Agile organizations make *effective* changes because they do a better job of selecting the ones that will deliver on environmental demands. Finally, agile organizations make *sustained* changes; after all, any change is meaningless unless the organization embeds it long enough to solve the problem it was intended to address.[1] However, the changes implemented do not become a permanent or institutionalized source of inertia; they are always subject to and ready for reform.

The management literature increasingly refers to this as a "dynamic capability"—the potential to sense opportunities and threats, solve problems, and change the firm's resources and processes.[2] This allows outperformers to maintain or enhance their relative advantages in ways their competitors fail to see or do not fully implement. Agility is also strategically relevant. Agile organizations often change, but they do not pursue change for change's sake. They pursue it for the sake of competitive advantage.

Four routines, summarized in Exhibit 2.1, distinguish outperformers from thrashers and underperformers. The ability to make timely, effective, and sustained change results from the capacity to

- *Strategize* in dynamic ways

- Accurately *perceive* changes in the external environment

EXHIBIT 2.1.   *The Routines of Agility*

Routine	Description
Strategizing	How top management teams establish an aspirational *purpose*, develop a widely shared *strategy*, and manage the climate and commitment to *execution*.
Perceiving	The process of broadly, deeply, and continuously monitoring the environment to *sense* changes and rapidly *communicate* these perceptions to decision makers, who *interpret* and formulate appropriate responses.
Testing	How the organization *sets up, runs, and learns from experiments*.
Implementing	How the organization maintains its *ability and capacity to implement changes*, both incremental and discontinuous, as well as its ability to *verify the contribution of execution* to performance.

Note: The exhibit describes organizational "routines." It would be a mistake to associate these with a particular structure or department, as in "this group does testing, that group does implementing."

- *Test* possible responses

- *Implement* changes in products, technology, operations, structures, systems, and capabilities as a whole

Individually, these routines draw from good management practice. However, the hard work necessary to orchestrate them for consistent high performance is advanced and uncommon. Most important, it is the whole system of routines—what we call the ITSS principle ("It's the system, stupid")—and not the possession of one or two of them that confers agility. By executing these routines in concert, over and over again, the outperformers consistently outpaced their competitors.

THE AGILITY PYRAMID

Agility is a high-order dynamic capability that is built over time on a solid foundation of good management practices and a set of differentiated capabilities that confer a competitive advantage, as shown in Exhibit 2.2.

At the base of the pyramid, most organizations are familiar with good management practices. They comprise the well-known principles associated with planning, organizing, directing, leading, and controlling an organization.[3] Good management involves, among other things,

EXHIBIT 2.2.   *The Agility Pyramid*

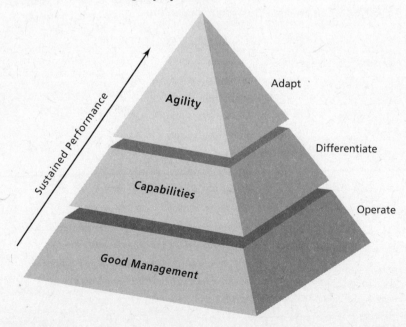

being able to formulate a strategy and objectives, develop capital and operating budgets, and reward employees in a systematic manner. Good management is a necessary condition for survival, but in itself it may not be sufficient. Many well-managed companies, such as Circuit City, Borders, R.H. Donnelly, and Bethlehem Steel, have disappeared for want of competitive advantage. Well-managed companies adopt best practices so they can be like the best but often end up being marginal performers because they lack competitive differentiation.

At the next level, organizations should be able to identify, develop, and implement a set of capabilities that differentiate them from competitors. Capabilities represent the ability and capacity of an organization to get things done. Some capabilities, such as lowering costs or improving quality, allow the organization to keep pace with a changing world. Other capabilities, such as designing superior customer experiences or opening new markets faster, can add value in distinct ways.

The development of differentiated capabilities draws on the resource-based view of strategy that suggests that competitive advantage can be achieved through the organization's resources and processes[4] (see "What Is the Resource-Based View?"). It also draws on organization design practice that views capabilities as the result of an integrated system of technology, structures, processes, and human capital.[5] The ability to develop and implement differentiated capabilities allows an organization to achieve better-than-average profitability.[6] Firms at this level of development want to be different so they can be better, faster, or cheaper than their competitors.

The cruel joke is that in attempting to preserve their source of advantage, organizations can overcommit to institutionalization, making them more inert and vulnerable to environmental shifts.

Most of the resource- and capabilities-based management bromides suggest that to achieve a sustainable competitive advantage, an organization must endeavor to preserve, protect, and defend its differentiated position. Resource-based views of strategy are full of suggestions about how to make advantages difficult to imitate by raising switching costs, keeping intellectual property secret, or developing new products more quickly. As a result, managers often hurry to make specific and, in some cases, large and irreversible commitments to sustain the advantage. The cruel joke is that in attempting to preserve their source of advantage,

WHAT IS THE RESOURCE-BASED VIEW?

The holy grail of strategy is a source of competitive advantage that can generate sustained, abnormally high profits. The resource-based view (RBV) of the firm is a branch of strategic management theory and research that posits that every firm can be viewed as a unique bundle of resources, including physical and financial assets, intellectual property, and human capital.[7] Under certain conditions, these resources can be a source of competitive advantage. Those conditions are that the resource be *valuable*, *rare*, *inimitable*, and *nonsubstitutable* (VRIN). If the resource is plentiful, it will be readily available to competitors. If it is easy to imitate, other firms will acquire or develop it and the source of advantage will be lost. The same holds true if substitutes for the resource can be found and exploited.

A refinement to the model came from an expanded definition of "resource." Resources include not only what a firm has, but also what it can do and how it goes about doing it. An important distinction has been made between resources, which may not be firm specific and can be traded, and routines, which are firm specific, not tradable, and rely on tacit knowledge. Routines are the regular and predictable behavior patterns in an organization.[8] They are developed and implemented mainly to improve reliability, increase efficiency, and support accountability for results within the firm.

An organizational capability is a high-level routine or collection of routines that, "together with its implementing input flows, confers upon an organization's management a set of decision options for producing significant outputs of a particular type."[9] Capabilities are also described as a bundle of know-how, processes, technology, and experience with the potential to confer competitive advantage. As such, capabilities are potentially VRIN. A firm's unique capacity to innovate (Apple), manufacture (Toyota), market (Procter & Gamble), or develop managerial talent (GE) can provide a source of competitive advantage that may be sustained for some time.

More recently, researchers have been writing about dynamic capabilities that confer a capacity to change in light of environmental requirements. Specifically, "a dynamic capability is the firm's potential to systematically solve problems, formed by its propensity to sense opportunities and threats, to make timely and market-oriented decisions, and to change its resource base."[10] *Ordinary* capabilities can provide competitive advantage if they are difficult to build and imitate. Once operational, they are also difficult to change. Dynamic capabilities provide a way to quickly and effectively modify the firm's resources to maintain a good environmental fit. As such, dynamic capabilities may represent the ultimate source of competitive advantage.

organizations can overcommit to institutionalization, making them more inert and vulnerable to environmental shifts.

Agile firms are not, in general, dependent on such practices or worried about such things, because they know that any competitive advantage is temporary.[11] If they do need to make large and relatively irreversible commitments, they think long and hard about it—longer and harder than may be recommended by traditional economic theory. Reflecting the best parts of the Japanese process of *nemawashi*, which builds commitment to change, agile firms are disciplined, rigorous, and patient. They may even appear slow and sluggish to outsiders because, knowing things will change, they carefully consider the balance between commitment and flexibility.

At the top of the pyramid, agility represents an institutionalized ability to do different things or do things differently when and where this creates a performance advantage for the firm. Their defining characteristic is the ability to make timely, effective, and sustained organization changes. Agile firms want to be adaptable so they can change more successfully than their competitors.

Agility represents an institutionalized ability to do things differently when and where this creates a performance advantage.

Our view of agility has been influenced by the population perspective (see "What Is Population Ecology?"). Agility replicates the Darwinian forces of variation, selection, and retention in the four routines of strategizing, perceiving, testing, and implementing. Unlike the random variations in organization evolution, responses to environmental challenges are managed purposefully and refined through experimentation. Unlike traditional organizations hamstrung by inertia, agile organizations can do this as quickly as environments change. The resulting adaptations in strategy, product/market mix, asset portfolio, capabilities, and so forth are chosen for their effectiveness. Agility enables companies to do this systematically, successfully, and repeatedly.

An important implication of this model is that as an organization develops, it can move up the pyramid from well-managed to differentiated, and from differentiated to agile. To do so, however, it must recast its management practices into a higher state of sophistication. In other words, applying the basic principles of good management is good enough until the organization embarks on differentiated capabilities. When an organization chooses to be better than its peers by developing

WHAT IS POPULATION ECOLOGY?

Population ecology, also known as organization ecology, is a branch of management theory and research that draws heavily on the biological concepts of Darwinian natural selection to explain how organizations survive, evolve, and change.[12] As with other organization theories, population ecologists believe that organizations succeed (survive) to the extent that the goods and services offered and the way they are produced fit with the requirements of the environment. Population ecology departs from more traditional theories in two important ways. First, the unit of study is a *population* of organizations (that is, an industry), not individual firms. Second, the theory holds that the *environment*, rather than managerial decisions, determines the number and form of organizations in a population at any particular time.

Like biological species, organizations are embedded in environments that consist mainly of other organizations, including competitors, suppliers, business customers, financial institutions, regulators, governments, and so on. Environments also include things like technology, economic and market conditions, geographic features, social attitudes, and other contextual factors that make production, distribution, delivery, and service provision easy or hard. Environments may be static or dynamic, uncertain or predictable, threatening or benign, but they always change, and with each change, the environment selects those organizations that best fit the new requirements. The environment determines—but does not care—whether larger organizations are better than smaller ones, generalists fare better than specialists, or multidivisional firms last longer than single business enterprises.

Population ecologists concede that organizations can try to adapt to the new requirements (what they call "variation") but argue that management's ability to do so is severely limited. First, it is difficult to predict the future, so managers cannot know with certainty what choices to make. Second, management's interest in sustaining performance under the old environmental demands leads them to develop formal bureaucratic procedures and investments in specific assets that increase the organization's reliability and accountability. The obsession with internal reliability and the uncertainty of knowing the environment creates organizational inertia and makes change risky, difficult, and costly.

Reading the population ecology research is very sobering for managers because it holds that the vast majority of attempts to adapt organizations to the changing needs of the environment are futile. As a result, the main source of variation in organization populations is new entrants and start-ups. The environment then selects the organizational forms that best fit. In general, there is a liability of newness—younger organizations are more likely to fail until they can achieve enough legitimacy and predictability to survive. On the other hand, no organization is "too big to fail," and mortality rates go up as firms age or try to transform themselves. Still, the processes of variation, selection, and retention operate on organizations just as they do in biological ecosystems.

And the population ecologists have the numbers to support their ideas. They have assembled impressive databases that span decades, sometimes centuries, showing that far more organizations have been "selected out" of populations by the environment than have adapted to changing requirements. In the early 1900s, there were over three hundred car makers in the United States. Where are they now? Competition for resources, technological advancement, regulatory change, and the breaching of environmental boundaries wreak havoc with even the most robust strategies.

Although population ecology may not offer much in the way of prescriptions or helpful advice for managers, it does provide an insightful and rigorous description of the power of environmental forces on organizations as well as a cautionary tale about the likelihood of long-term survival. As Hannan and Freeman, the fathers of the population ecology school, put it: "Learning and adjusting structure enhances the chance of survival only if the speed of response is commensurate with the temporal patterns of relevant environments....Can organizations learn about their environments and change strategies and structures as quickly as their environments change? If the answer is negative, replacement or selection arguments are potentially applicable."[13]

However, if organizations can be designed to learn and change faster, then adaptation has a fighting chance.

differentiated capabilities, it must add some elements of good management and enhance some others. For example, good management includes crafting plans and holding people accountable for results. When building and executing differentiated capabilities, good management must take organizational learning into account. The management system must now be able to measure whether a capability delivers value in excess of its costs, if that value is increasing, through learning, or not, and take actions based on those results. They are the same systems, but they are designed to support a higher level of organizational functioning.

Adding or enhancing management processes as an organization pursues agility is especially important in the area of leadership practices. Many of the agility routines depend on a climate of openness, challenge, and debate, or what O'Toole and Bennis refer to as a "culture of candor."[14] Whereas good management traditionally defines leadership as a level in the hierarchy (that is, leadership is what senior executives do) and differentiated organizations define leadership as a personal trait (that is, we need to develop more leaders), agile organizations define leadership as an organization capacity (that is, leadership responsibility is shared throughout the organization).

As moments arise when the right thing to do is uncertain or when something needs to be challenged, agile organizations need individuals to come forward and provide leadership. They need to be effective in resolving conflicts, making trade-offs, and getting the right things done to achieve results or make changes. This will happen only if the organization develops and supports a leadership philosophy of shared responsibility. Agile organizations work properly when all employees know the strategy and are aware of the environment, are expected to "speak truth to power," and take the initiative to get work done. We will see this aspect of good management come up repeatedly in the following chapters.

The big difference in the step up from differentiated capabilities to agility is that good management practices must not only support differentiation, they must also be dynamic and flexible (Exhibit 2.3). The systems that supported organization survival and effective competition must now be designed to change easily. In fact, establishing agility as a viable concept is difficult because, even as the world is changing faster and faster, the market often rewards companies for reliably delivering today's results. Organizations that are rewarded for institutionalizing effective capabilities often feel betrayed by environmental change. The clear but uncomfortable realization is that sustainable performance requires reliability *and* innovation, exploitation *and* exploration, stability *and* change.[15]

DAVITA

DaVita is the kidney dialysis division of DaVita HealthCare Partners, a Fortune 500 health care services organization. Before the acquisition of the HealthCare Partners physician practice in 2012, the dialysis organization *was* the business. DaVita is one of the few organizations we have found that not only operates as an agile organization but transformed itself to agile.

EXHIBIT 2.3. *Agility Is Good Management Reconsidered*

	Agile	Differentiated	Good Management
Outperformer Be adaptable — change more effectively than the rest	• Can operate flexible resource allocation system • Manages complex learning and change capabilities • Comfortable with ambidextrous focus	• Shifts from one capability set to another • Controls two sets of capabilities — one focused on current results and one focused on developing future strategies • Learning is single and double loop	• Planning is scenario based and dynamic • Controlling is through "rolling" (quarterly) forecasts • Organizing is sophisticated and network based • Leading is an organization capacity
Thrasher Be different — be better than the rest		• Connects internal resources with external opportunities • Sees capability as an organization design problem • Learning is primarily single loop	• Planning is driven by environment and resources • Controlling is through budgets and commitment • Organizing through decentralization and team-based systems • Leading is a personal trait to be developed, especially in high potentials
Survivor Be like the best — adopt best practices			• Planning is static and linear • Controlling is through annual budgets • Organizing through centralization and hierarchy • Leading is the responsibility of the top levels

Prelude to a Transformation

Founded in 1979 as Medical Ambulatory Care as part of National Medical Enterprises (NME, now Tenet Healthcare), Total Renal Care (TRC) spun off from NME in 1994 and went public in 1995, offering kidney dialysis treatments in thirty-seven outpatient facilities and twenty-eight inpatient hospital contracts.[16] The IPO provided TRC's CEO, Victor Chaltiel, with the cash to pursue an aggressive acquisition and growth strategy.

This strategy made a lot of sense. First, the industry was fragmented. In 1992, the seven largest dialysis providers controlled only 30 percent of industry capacity. Outpatient dialysis facilities were usually owned and operated by groups of nephrologists, or by hospitals that were trying to outsource the management of their dialysis facilities. Second, in a macabre way, an aging population, increased obesity, and more sedentary lifestyles made treating end-stage renal disease (ESRD) a growth industry. The number of patients requiring dialysis in the United States increased at a 9 percent compounded annual rate during Chaltiel's tenure, jumping from sixty-six thousand in 1982 to two hundred thousand in 1995. Finally, the roll-up strategy was familiar to Chaltiel. He had learned the model of leveraging cost savings obtained through large-scale purchasing and distribution systems for drugs in the Medicare reimbursement program in a prior organization. His focus on growth through acquisition through the 1990s—in the context of the dot-com bubble, during which many analysts were focused on topline revenue growth—provided TRC with a high stock price that allowed it to continue making acquisitions at a fast pace.

By the end of 1996, the company had more than doubled its size and controlled a network of 134 outpatient facilities and 59 inpatient management agreements. In November 1997, the company acquired its closest competitor, Renal Treatment Centers, for $1.3 billion in stock, and nearly doubled TRC's size again, while also establishing a global footprint with centers in Guam, Puerto Rico, Argentina, and Europe. In a November 24, 1997, interview with *Modern Healthcare*, Chaltiel's goal was clear: "We will now have the critical mass necessary to ensure our position as the leading independent provider of dialysis services in the United States and the resources to rapidly expand."[17]

Although the strategy may have been sound, senior executives paid little attention to the dialysis centers and the operational requirements of the business. They failed to deliver the improved quality and economies of scale required of a roll-up strategy. For example, work methods across centers were not standardized, and there were few systems to record and monitor patient care during dialysis. To make matters worse, TRC's insurance reimbursement process was not well organized or operated. Private insurers and Medicare/Medicaid frequently questioned charges and demanded additional documentation. Occasionally they unilaterally reduced the reimbursement amount or delayed payment until they received the requested documentation.

The situation deteriorated after the Renal Treatment Centers acquisition. The sudden doubling of the company's patient and staff base put a strain on its infrastructure and the six-hundred-person billing and bookkeeping office in Tacoma, Washington. Accounts went uncollected, patients were billed incorrectly, and the reimbursement process failed to support the larger network. Instead of being seen as the source of value-add, the dialysis centers were simply an indicator of size— economic units in a bigger financial structure—and the financial orientation of TRC's management did little to provide a motivating environment for the people working in the field.

As a result of the inefficient processes, squeezed resources, and the increased debt load (reaching $1.5 billion in 1999), cash flow quickly became a serious problem. In spring of 1999, the company announced that its earnings would fall short of expectations, and the company defaulted on its loans. The stock fell from a high of $50 to $2 a share. Before the year ended, Chaltiel and the company's chief financial officer resigned. One analyst referred to the Chaltiel-led organization as "a disaster of a company. All they did was buy things instead of focus on running the company."[18]

The Transformation of DaVita

When Kent Thiry took over as CEO in 1999, he launched a transformation that had two vectors: fix the business and build the culture. On the business side, his new management team and a new board of directors negotiated with their lenders to obtain a new line of credit, giving the company some financial breathing room. They invested in information systems and divested nearly all of the company's international operations.

In parallel with the business turnaround, Thiry, the Chief Operating Officer Joe Mello, and their colleagues understood that what they said and did in those first months would set the culture of the organization for years. They immediately recast the organization's mission and purpose. "The previous company was almost exclusively focused on shareholders, and our new mission is to be the provider, partner, and employer of choice. We realize that we have to satisfy our shareholders with a reasonable return, but that is not our primary mission."

In May of 2000, more than four hundred clinic managers and corporate staff assembled in Phoenix, Arizona—appropriately, reflecting the bird that rose from the ashes—for the first of what would become an annual corporate-wide meeting. During the meeting, suggestions for a new name for the company were presented. It was the assembled employees, called "teammates," not the board or the senior management, who voted on and chose the new name. In an industry where 20 percent of customers die each year, they decided to call the company DaVita, Italian for "to give life." Small groups also discussed, debated, and voted on proposals for the core values that would guide the firm. Exhibit 2.4 shows the mission statement and core values selected by the Phoenix delegation.[19]

EXHIBIT 2.4. *DaVita's Mission and Values*

Our Mission

To Be The
Provider,
Partner And
Employer
Of choice

Our Core Values

Service Excellence
Integrity
Team
Continuous Improvement
Accountability
Fulfillment
Fun

Subsequently, the organization thought hard about its way of managing and has captured many of the principles in a set of phrases—a short and easily remembered mission, "new, ours, special," and GSD (short for "get stuff done"). These values, principles, and the associated behaviors are incorporated into interview protocols used to select new teammates, performance appraisals, and the company employee attitude and satisfaction surveys.

For example, DaVita gatherings routinely begin with executives asking those assembled to respond to three questions: "What is this company? Whose company is it? What could it be?" The answers, shouted back, are "new," "ours," and "special." DaVita was a new and different organization after the 2000 turnaround, and it was important that everyone understood that DaVita was not going to stand still. DaVita was always going to be a "new" company, constantly reinventing itself. "Ours" meant that the company is the responsibility of and under the control of the teammates who work for it, who have the opportunity to make the company what they would like it to be. This leads to the last question. Executives do not ask "What *is* the company?" but rather "What *could* it be?" The answer, "Special," captures in a word the aspirations for building an organization that is truly unique in its culture and patient focus. The "could be" reflects the fact that the development of the organization is a journey, and although it has achieved great things, its aspirations are for more, and being special is something yet to be realized.

The DaVita management approach also emphasizes execution. Every executive on Kent Thiry's management team had experienced organizations full of talented and hardworking people that never got anything done, and they were determined not to let that happen at DaVita. At another off-site meeting, they concluded that there were four elements critical for effective execution: (1) absolute clarity of purpose, (2) absolute accountability, (3) relentless follow-up, and (4) the celebration of success. These principles and practices helped build operational excellence and an ability to get things done at DaVita, where they were very much a part of the fabric of the management approach. In fact, recognition of the ability to GSD (get stuff done) was considered high praise indeed.

By 2004, DaVita ranked as the second-largest provider of dialysis services in the United States, trailing only Germany's Fresenius Medical Care in size. In December 2004, DaVita acquired Gambro Healthcare in a $3 billion deal that would combine DaVita's 664 clinics with Gambro Healthcare's 565 clinics. It temporarily created the largest U.S. dialysis services company, until Fresenius responded by acquiring Renal Care Group in May 2005.

Building Agility at DaVita

The DaVita story is a great example of building an agile organization from the ground up. Clearly, the TRC organization was not able to demonstrate good management. While their environmental scanning, strategy formulation, and acquisition practices might have passed muster, their execution of the roll-up strategy was a complete failure. In contrast, Thiry and his thirty-three thousand teammates have put in place an organization that is built to change and sustain performance. Today, DaVita possesses the four broad routines of agility that we will describe in the upcoming chapters. Although no organization is perfect —sometimes even agile organizations need to fix their basic management processes or shift their differentiated capabilities—DaVita's history gives us a concrete example of good management, capabilities, and the routines of agility.

Strategizing Dynamically

Few would argue that a clear, powerful, and shared strategy is an important, well-accepted principle of good management. However, agile organizations don't define strategy the way other firms do. Some organizations readily admit they don't have a strategy. Others point to aggressive-sounding goals listed in a balanced scorecard or declare strategies that are really goals in disguise: "Our strategy is to be #1 in our market." Still others point to the outputs of annual strategic planning processes or refer to mission, vision, and value statements that supposedly guide decision making.

Agile firms use a set of strategy concepts to create a context of competition and change. A mission or purpose outlines the company's aspirations, while strategy describes the nature of today's competitive advantage, the means used to achieve success in the past and likely to achieve success in the future, and the values and behaviors that guide decisions. They are careful to define strategy with change in mind and to describe how the organization engages in a competitive space. In short, an agile organization's view of strategy is more dynamic.

As soon as Kent Thiry (most often referred to as KT) was hired as CEO of DaVita, he talked about the mission of being the "provider, partner, and employer of choice," a phrase still used a lot today. As the leadership team thought about building the new organization and culture, a more sophisticated way of thinking about strategy emerged, guided by several principles—some that change all the time and some that don't. In mid-2011, Thiry described what he saw as the four "rings" to DaVita's strategy:

> First, our vision is to be the greatest kidney dialysis company the world has ever seen. Second, we are a village first and a company second—we are a village and all that the metaphor implies. Third, we want to be a role model for American health care. The system is broken and until we fix the delivery system, we are going to be in trouble. We can be a leader in that. Finally, we want to send forth ripples of citizen leadership—we want to be good citizens, and you cannot separate who you are from what you do at work.

This definition of strategy reflects several important features that most agile firms use to both compete and change. First, the GDC vision (short for "greatest dialysis company") is, like the mission statement, aspirational. In some ways it can never be achieved, because you can always be better. The "new, ours, special" mantra complements this vision and keeps the organization moving forward. Second, the organization is very clear about who it is, what inspires it, and how it behaves to be successful. A senior VP told us, "If you asked me, 'What is the organization strategy?' I'd say the ends that we have are clear: to be a village first and company second. In a village, it takes having a healthy business to support the village." This is DaVita's identity, a unique concept in our theory of agility and a statement that serves multiple purposes.

An identity describes the character of the organization. It teaches people how and why the organization has been successful in the past, provides a "North Star" for how and why the organization will make strategic choices in the future, and provides the foundation for why the organization sees change as a natural feature of organizational life. Being a village first and a company second describes how and why the organization has been successful in the past. DaVita believes that its success has been a direct result of taking care of each other, their patients, and their communities—the village. DaVita also believes that being a village first and a company second is the North Star that guides choices and decisions about the future. When teammates and executives are faced with difficult choices about what to do, the organization's identity provides an important rule: Do what's best for the village. One member of top management explained:

> I've been in big public health care company conversations where we were always talking about what we were going to do to drive stock performance for the quarter. We never have that conversation at DaVita. I asked KT why we don't talk about that, and he said, "If you do this [patient care and quality] and that [take care of teammates' quality of life], then stock price will happen."

Being a village first and a company second encourages people and sets the expectation for change. Any healthy village is evolving and growing, so what it has to do today is different from what it had to do yesterday.

There is a clear line of sight to the business in the third ring. The U.S. health care system is broken, and DaVita has taken on the responsibility of being part of the cure by focusing on the operation of the dialysis centers. For example, early in the transformation, the new philosophy recognized that the centers, where patient care was delivered and where most people worked, were keys to the company's success. To emphasize the importance of the centers, Thiry and all his senior managers "adopted" centers and spent significant time there. One member of the executive team at DaVita described the vital role of the centers as follows:

> We are so focused on clinical outcomes. We are a public company, for sure, but every day when we start, we start with taking care of 120,000 people who are very sick. Our 30,000 teammates are different because they are caregivers and because they recognize that the company puts the patients ahead of everything…When you get that part right, it drives performance—good care drives outcomes, brings in the best people, people make better decisions, docs say that DaVita takes better care of my patients. We have a 3 percent lower mortality rate than any other firm and when you add that up, it's a big deal.

This is the essence of DaVita's strategic intent. They understand very well that a successful dialysis company must comply with stringent government regulations and deliver high-quality clinical and operational outcomes. Compliance means keeping meticulous records on all aspects of patient care and service delivery so that the right forms can be filled out the right way and submitted in a timely fashion.

Delivering high-quality clinical and operational outcomes relies on a delicate balance of efficiency and human resource management. An efficient center can affect both operational and clinical outcomes. Operational results depend on small but important behaviors and decisions, such as carefully using supplies to avoid waste, actively maintaining material inventories, properly reusing dialysis filters, and maintaining the dialysis machines to ensure both long equipment life and lower cost per treatment. If a company performs seven million dialysis treatments in a year, each .01 hour savings in labor per treatment is worth about $1.8 million to the bottom line. Attention to detail also matters a lot for obtaining good clinical outcomes. For example, it is important to take care during all three fundamental steps: putting the patient on the machine, monitoring the treatment as it is occurring, and taking the patient off the machine at the end of the session.

Good human resource management is a second contributor to clinical and operational outcomes. Achieving good clinical outcomes depends to a large extent on the patient's commitment to treatment, which in turn depends on the emotional relationship with the dialysis center and its caregivers. If a center can create a supportive climate, those positive emotions can improve patient attitudes, commitment to treatments, and survival, or at least the patients' quality of life. On the operations side, labor costs represent about one-third to one-half of the treatment costs, and dialysis companies are in fierce competition with other health care service providers for scarce nursing talent. Overtime costs required by covering for open positions can destroy the economics of a center. Similarly, high turnover impairs outcomes because a technician's experience in doing dialysis and working in a team enhances patient care outcomes.

Finally, there's a purpose—creating ripples of citizen leadership—that transcends growth and profitability. DaVita sees no conflict in being a good business and a good corporate citizen. As one executive put it, "[The people who were here at the beginning] got the mission and values right, and...putting those things up front 90 to 95 percent of the time has been a huge reason for our success. We live by those values, and it forces us to do the right thing."

Perhaps most important of all, everybody in the organization knows all this. In interviews, in public presentations, in award ceremonies, in meetings, and in their day-to-day interactions among the people at DaVita, they are discussing and applying these principles, ideas, words, and phrases. Like many successful companies, DaVita has been criticized for its cultlike culture. An executive recalls his recruitment by DaVita:

> KT used words that I was thinking about: Is this community first, village stuff real? They [DaVita] are performing so well, do they really believe this stuff? I was intrigued enough and the ideas fit me personally, but it had to be real. Ultimately I concluded that it was real, and more importantly, there are some pretty good business practices that support it all.

Perceiving Environmental Change

Agile companies take care to sense what is going on in the environment—short, medium, and long term—through multiple touch points and structural choices that put managers and employees in direct contact with customers, regulators, and other stakeholders. They are skilled at communicating those sensations to decision makers in the company in unbiased and unfiltered ways, and they have the support and knowledge they need to interpret those messages as important or unimportant, opportunity or threat. All three elements are essential. Sensing without communicating is waste; communicating without interpreting is noise.

DaVita monitors the environment with an eye on both the long term and short term. It's a very strategic company. Top management told us that, "There's a strong view toward what's happening five years, ten years down the road. For example, 80 percent of our patients are government reimbursement, and so we spend a lot of time and presence to build credibility in Washington, D.C. As a result, we are in conversations with the people who are making the legislation that will affect the future." In addition, the organization charters teams that look to drive future value for the company, build leaders, research the implications of health care reform, identify M&A prospects, and develop new business.

They also stay close to the customer. Each local dialysis center attends to the needs of patients, physicians, and the community. That information is moved up the hierarchy by the "town hall" process, as a member of the executive team notes:

> If you walk into a clinic, an exec must do a town hall. It's a formal way to get information from the bottom up. They can ask anything they want to, and we do it at the national meetings as well. Information from these town hall gatherings has caused us to slow things down or change something we are doing. The expectation is that if you hear things, you will bring it up and follow it up. If a team member asks you a question that you don't know the answer to, you say you will get back to them and you'd better do it or you'll hear about it.

All that information—from dialysis centers and meetings—is funneled to top management for consideration. But if you ask, "Who's on the top management team?" you'll get a puzzled look. At DaVita, different top management teams are accountable for different purposes. This allows them to put the right people with the right expertise on various issues, and it improves their ability to interpret signals from their externally focused organization.

To keep all employees focused on the external environment, DaVita abandoned the organization chart. When we ask DaVita managers to present at a conference, class, or seminar, we always ask them to be sure to talk about the organization structure. And they always do; they show a blank slide. As Thiry says, "We don't have an organization chart—it's not who you report to—it's what you are accountable for." From his point of view, structure focuses too much attention on the hierarchy, on who's your boss, and whom you should look to for guidance, and not enough on understanding your responsibility, the local marketplace, or the broader environment. To DaVita's way of thinking, asking people to worry about the politics of hierarchy would be intentionally placing a barrier in front of their ability to pursue the "new, ours, special" mantra and destroy the village. Says one senior manager: "It's easy to become large, layered, and full of hierarchy and titles. But we have few titles, strange titles, and groups that are dynamic. We keep a fluid management team, our metrics are fluid, and there's intellectual integrity involved."

Testing Responses

What does DaVita do with all the data generated by the external focus of its perceiving routine? "We run a lot of experiments," said one senior executive. Agile organizations have internal processes for taking insights from the perceiving routine, developing innovations, and trying something to see if it works. These testing activities can range from gathering further intelligence, to process improvement, to trying out new ideas on a small scale, to large product development programs.

> *The value of nimbleness must exceed the cost of chaos.*
>
> —Kent Thiry, CEO, DaVita

When the testing routine is focused on large-scale innovation and big risks, it tolerates a good deal of the right kind of failures. It's important to understand that agile companies apply explicit risk management processes with clear success criteria so the plug can be pulled if a test fails. They invest significantly in learning and continuous improvement, never resting on their laurels or believing they have "cracked the code" once and for all. These rigorous learning efforts allow the insights gained from the tests to spread to all relevant parts of the company.

Thiry explains:

> There has to be a tolerance for change and waste. Executives can get frustrated with the redundancy...it's an old mind-set that they use to judge the effectiveness of a system or organization. Having a "fast break" offense implies more turnovers than another kind of offensive strategy—you are pushing harder. My job as leader is to make sure people are sensitive to "net" efficiency and effectiveness. The value of nimbleness must exceed the cost of chaos.

At DaVita, experiments related to the core business are usually handed over to operations, where a tighter continuous improvement process has a narrower definition of success and less tolerance for failure. The "chief wisdom officer" told us,

> If there are new practices and policies or procedures, we'll do pilots in areas or centers, learn from that, and apply it in a full-scale rollout. We do a lot of learning this way and with a lot of different types of changes. This small-scale approach helps to identify the unintended consequences. [That is,] we almost always believe that

we have thought through everything, and then we get surprised. And what's important about that is that if you find something, you are expected to make the changes no matter what you think is best. We'll change something 180 degrees if we have to. It's a guiding principle. It makes it acceptable to go down a different path.

This investment in testing, failing, experimenting, innovating, and learning suggests that agile organizations are not always and everywhere "lean and mean." They have flexible resource allocation systems and consciously build in organizational slack—people, money, and time—that doesn't go directly to the bottom line. Rather, it allows an agile organization to rapidly deploy resources against opportunities that may or may not pay off, without jeopardizing day-to-day operations. Higher staffing levels can also play an important role in capturing and disseminating learning that the organization can use later. This is how Thiry described it for DaVita: "We have what we call 'village scouts,' talented people with strong backgrounds that get deployed as utility players, ready to work on any important project as it comes up. These people are resources for sharing."

Nimbleness is about concentrated time, not elapsed time.

When asked, "Don't the financial analysts think that's inefficient?" Thiry responded,

From one point of view, yes, but it's better than having a particular function with a dedicated resource that gets fully used 50 percent of the time and underused 50 percent of the time. These sharp people move around to focus attention and resources on the initiatives that need support. It's related to "concentrated time."

Nimbleness is about concentrated time, not elapsed time. If something is really important and it will take a hundred hours to complete, then why distract someone from getting that important thing done in a hundred hours by giving them two other important things to do? The really important thing will get done in two months instead of a hundred hours because the person has to switch back and forth between multiple priorities.

To make sure they are leveraging concentrated time, DaVita uses the Accountability and Resource Chart (ARC) to keep track of initiatives and priorities and to develop key talent. The "Murphy Team" (Thiry and some senior managers) spends about 20 percent of its time "staring" at the ARC and asking, "Are we resourced correctly for the short and long term?" What they "stare" at is a table of current projects (*Are these the right initiatives to be working on?*) and the extent to which each project has (1) the right clarity in terms of a shared purpose and plan and metric, (2) the right leader with enough capacity to do the job, (3) the right resources, and (4) the right learning processes. Joe Mello commented on the ARC:

> ARC is a very dynamic document, and there are a few subtleties. For example, it's listed in alphabetical order by people, not titles. Second, there are names on there that are not at senior levels; there are some executives but also others from throughout the organization. It's not an issue of titles, it's about who's responsible for what (projects and functions). There is also a "parking lot" of stuff that is waiting to be assigned, not currently a priority.

Kent Thiry continued:

> One of my biggest learnings early on was that often your best people don't want to do new things. People who are leading and managing large successful businesses often want to keep doing that or doing it better or whatever. Most new stuff—and a key to nimbleness—is that things start small and don't look all that sexy. It's important to set up the right and proper incentives and make it glamorous enough to get the best people working on the new stuff. The ARC helps us do that.

Implementing Change

Finally, agile companies have mastered the program management capabilities they need to scale up the successful tests, promising innovations, and new capabilities required by new strategies. Their organizations are flexible enough to implement them with commitment, speed, and impact. Agile companies have histories of successful transformations, restructurings, and merger integrations, and they excel at the execution of new product rollouts, policy changes, and compliance mandates. As one executive told us:

> How many lives has this organization had? From (1) a rollup to (2) a turnaround to (3) a stable operating company to (4) the best dialysis company to (5) a doubling in size with the Gambro acquisition. There's been a fair amount of change, and with each shift in phases there have been changes in the required competencies, skill

sets, management processes. We've gone, for example, from five hundred different processes to one way of delivering care. Yeah, we do change.

The successful implementation of change relies on competent, well-managed talent, a shared leadership philosophy, and a change capability that is not relegated to a staff function at headquarters. Rather, the resources and processes of change are embedded in line and staff organizations. Once a decision is made, managers charged with implementation are monitored, but not second-guessed, by top management teams. According to a senior executive:

We actually [implement changes] all the time. The reason we have no organization chart is so we don't have to worry about it. We don't have to go through hierarchy to get something done or to create a team. We don't care about structure; we care about accountability. What's the project, what's the deliverable we want? We don't care about titles. We put the right people on the team, and we go.

Agile organizations also are good at continuously improving, but they are not constrained to a single view of learning. They recognize that any routine can be a source of both stability and change.[20] In the early days of DaVita's transformation, Joe Mello set up the "B52" process to improve operational, clinical, or people performance and satisfaction. At the time, there were roughly 520 centers, and for any measure on the dashboard, they identified the bottom 10 percent (hence the term B52, for bottom 52 centers). This group participated in weekly calls with Mello and Thiry until they were no longer on the B52 list for that dimension of performance. The process was not punitive, although you definitely did not want to be on any B52 list. In the call, the centers would share best practices, describe their improvement plans, and openly discuss barriers that needed to be overcome. The B52 process committed the organization to a focus on clinical and operational performance improvement.

When continuous improvement is only a process to make things more predictable and reliable, and when the pursuit of that objective becomes paramount, continuous improvement becomes an untouchable and sacred process and the only type of learning that is seen as valuable. Agile organizations are good at double loop learning, as well as single loop learning (such as continuous improvement).[21] The external focus of the perceiving routine prevents the organization from getting locked into a situation where it is perfecting the wrong process or believing that a work process will never have to be swapped out for a wholly new technology. They are open to changing the assumptions on which they operate. As a member of DaVita's top management told us,

> We are very thoughtful about what we ask the centers to do. In each center, prominently displayed when you walk in the door, is the DQI—the Davita Quality Index…not earnings per share or revenue growth. We keep them focused on delivery and outcomes, and we don't distract them. We do a good job of setting up alpha and beta pilots to try new things; we build new centers every year, and so we can try new procedures before people get tied into ways of doing things. We're very big and committed to CQI [continuous quality improvement] in the centers, business levels, IT, etc. Our teams are very cross-functional.

To execute all this change well requires returning to good management practices and designing them with change in mind. The implementing routine is the primary driver of current performance and typically occupies most of the people in an organization. It must therefore be supported by the most rigorous and flexible talent management systems possible.

At DaVita, and in line with GSD, there is a strong performance management system that encourages accountability, but the system of accountability goes far beyond the formal practice and is reinforced by the culture. For example, performance targets are objective and unambiguous, and positive and negative consequences are real and transparent. Thiry says,

> Our view is that in order to evaluate someone, you need four things: (1) What were their numbers and results? (2) What momentum are they carrying into next year? (3) Are they building a better "balance sheet" in terms of being a village leader [mentoring others], and so on and (4) What is the degree of difficulty?

A senior manager continued, "Just because you set a goal doesn't mean that when it's time to judge things, they are locked in stone. Degree of difficulty counts. If we say the goal today is a 2 and it should have been a 6, you don't get much credit for getting a 3."

Human capital must be developed and incented to not only deliver current results but to change as well. To encourage results, DaVita relies heavily on a profit sharing reward system. One member of the executive team told us, "Everything here has been thought about carefully. For example, profit sharing is completely discretionary and totally flexible. We've spent a lot more in profit sharing than in any 401(k) match program, but this is so much more flexible. Everything is tied to the concept of the village…if the village makes a profit, we share.…If it makes a lot of profit, a lot gets shared, but if things are down, we are all down and everybody understands."

In addition to results, a teammate's overall performance review is significantly weighted by their support of the mission, vision, and values. On a scale of 1 to 5, they are rated on the statement "leads by example in words, deeds, and behaviors." Senior managers' support of the mission, vision, and values is called out in detail. Executives are scored on their commitment to the mission—becoming the provider, partner, and employer of choice—as well as the seven values. Thus DaVita's performance management system incents both results and the way those results are achieved.

The ITSS Principle

Most people have heard of the KISS principle, which means "Keep it simple, stupid." The development of an agile capability is largely a function of the ITSS principle: "It's the system, stupid." Executives recognize that agility is the result of an integrated set of routines. No single resource, routine, or capability can sustain performance; only a system of resources, routines, and capabilities working, changing, and learning together can do this. The more agility routines the organization has and the more they complement each other, the higher the level of performance.[22] The sustained levels of profitability we reported in Chapter One are directly related to the organization's implementation of the routines. As shown in Exhibit 2.5 and based on the survey described in the Preface, when an organization's scores on three or four of the routines are above the average of the sample, they are significantly more likely to have an outperformance pattern.[23]

DaVita's scores on these four routines are significantly higher than those of the other firms in our sample (Exhibit 2.6). Its effective perceiving routine feeds new and future ideas into its strategizing process as well as into its testing and implementing routines. People and other resources are flexibly allocated to the highest-priority initiatives to look for and test ideas even while most people are concentrating on and improving the dialysis treatment process. It all works together because it was designed to work together: everything supporting both effectiveness and change, always focused on being a village first, a company second, and making everything new, ours, special.

As a result, since the turnaround DaVita has sustained its above-average profitability (Exhibit 2.7), slipping only when it made the Gambro and HealthPartners acquisitions and when the industry had a spectacular year.

EXHIBIT 2.5. *Agile Routines and Sustained Performance*

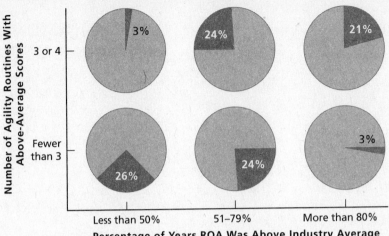

Number of Agility Routines With Above-Average Scores

3 or 4 — 3% | 24% | 21%

Fewer than 3 — 26% | 24% | 3%

Less than 50% | 51–79% | More than 80%

Percentage of Years ROA Was Above Industry Average

EXHIBIT 2.6. *DaVita's Agility Scores*[24]

	Strategizing	Perceiving	Testing	Implementing
DaVita	Significantly Above Average	Significantly Above Average	Significantly Above Average	Significantly Above Average

EXHIBIT 2.7. *DaVita Profitability Pattern*

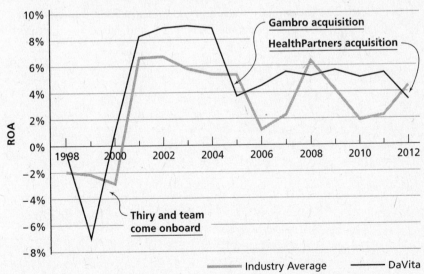

Gambro acquisition

HealthPartners acquisition

Thiry and team come onboard

ROA

1998 2000 2002 2004 2006 2008 2010 2012

━━━ Industry Average   ━━━ DaVita

Note: The industry average comprises firms active over this fourteen-year period in the ICB 4533 subsector of health care services. It includes dialysis, diagnostic, imaging, and laboratory services but does not include hospitals, dentists, clinics, or health maintenance organizations.

CONCLUSION

Agility is a dynamic capability that allows an organization to make timely, effective, and sustained changes repeatedly. In the Agility Pyramid, we positioned this capability as an advanced organization capacity that rests on a solid foundation of good management practices and differentiated capabilities. While good management allows the organization to operate well, and differentiated capabilities allow the organization to perform well in the current period, it is agility that allows the organization to make the changes necessary to sustain performance over time. The agile capability comprises four routines—strategizing, perceiving, testing, and implementing—that are explored more deeply in the next two chapters.

CHAPTER

3

STRATEGIZING AND PERCEIVING

Fortune favors the prepared mind.

—LOUIS PASTEUR

As the first decade of the new millennium drew to a close, Nokia was riding high on a series of smart choices and preparing to capture the next wave of mobile convergence. In late 2008, Nokia acquired the remaining 52 percent of Symbian that it did not already own for about $410 million in cash. Following this purchase, Nokia reorganized the UK-based mobile software company as a not-for-profit foundation to license its mobile operating system on a *royalty-free* basis to other cell phone manufacturers, which included Samsung, Motorola, and Sony Ericsson. The move was part of a strategy to democratize the cell phone marketplace.

Also in 2008, Nokia broke out its Nokia Siemens Networks business and acquired the digital mapping and navigation software provider NAVTEQ. This $8.1 billion acquisition was made to improve Nokia's ability to enhance the feature set of its mobile devices in response to increased competition in the smartphone market, where navigation features were becoming standard. In fact, Nokia had been playing with the idea of integrated cell phone and internet services since the late 1990s. One popular story described Anssi Vanjoki, then the EVP of markets, wandering in the woods in 2002 with an early version of GPS and real-izing how critical an understanding of where you are—what he called "context"—would be to an online experience.

Despite a few speed bumps along the way, since 1998 Nokia had maintained a worldwide leading market share that was consistently north of 30 percent, and it was clearly moving to position itself for the future. For example, Nokia created the Ovi Store to sell applications in August 2007. These were heady times, and there was barely a twitter about the impending global financial crisis. As one business writer put it: "Nokia...has a history of reinventing itself even when times are good."[1]

But everyone knows the story from here. The recession that began in December 2007 was tough on Nokia (see Exhibit 3.1). Not only did its high-volume, low-margin business in emerging markets come to a halt, but the slowdown in the North American market exposed Nokia's lack of progress in the region and allowed Apple to press its "hip" image and technology advantage with the launch of the iPhone and its subse-quent incarnations. Over the next few years, Nokia lost its global market share lead to Samsung, did not compete well in the smartphone segment, and failed to build an "app" ecosystem, all critical issues for a firm with high fixed costs. As Nokia's market share, profits, share price, and

EXHIBIT 3.1. *Nokia's ROA Performance 1994–2009*

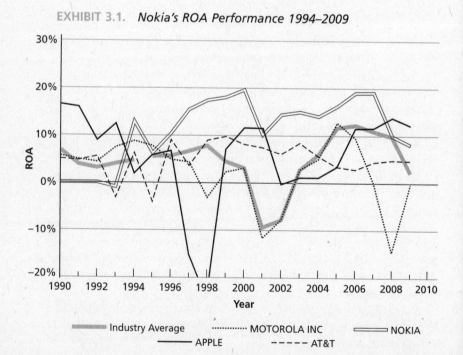

reputation were challenged, the organization made a CEO change, asking Stephen Elop to succeed Olli-Pekka Kallasvuo in September 2010. "It's the crossroads," said the president of Nokia North America. "We're at a pivotal moment, another moment like paper to rubber to electronics to devices to solutions/apps." In 2013, Nokia sold its mobile devices business to Microsoft for $7.2 billion.

Shortly after his arrival in 2010, Elop described Nokia's goals and strategy. The organization would address perceptions, both internal and external, that it had become a bit slower and less agile. First, Nokia planned to regain its position as an important player in the smartphone category. To do that, they announced a strategic partnership with Microsoft in February 2011. Its first product, the Lumia 900, was introduced just seven months later. The Smart Devices group (see Exhibit 3.2), in partnership with Microsoft, was charged with building a global mobile ecosystem that would provide a third alternative to the Apple and Android marketplaces. As Elop said in a memo famously leaked to the press, strategy in the telecom space had shifted: "The battle of devices has now become a war of ecosystems."

Second, Nokia sought to regain market share globally. The Mobile Phones group would focus on bringing modern and affordable mobile experiences to people around the world and would leverage its

EXHIBIT 3.2. *Nokia Organization in 2011–12*

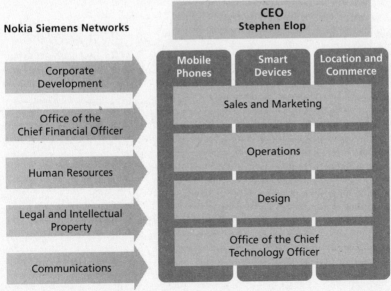

innovation and strength in growth markets to connect even more people to their first internet and application experience. Nokia believed that a compelling, affordable, and localized mobile experience, particularly in emerging markets, could bring the next billion people online. The Nokia Siemens Networks organization would continue to provide telecommunications infrastructure hardware, software, and services in support of that objective.

Third, Nokia would invest in its platform, software, and applications assets to bring "the next" mobile experience to consumers and enable business opportunities for developers. The Location & Commerce business would develop a range of location-based products and services for consumers (such as NAVTEQ), as well as platform services and local commerce services for device manufacturers, application developers, internet services providers, merchants, and advertisers.

THE STRATEGIZING ROUTINE

Images of agility conjure up nimble moves, quick responses to changing conditions, and swift execution of strategic initiatives. Apple's preemption of the digital music or mobile phone markets; Microsoft's Kinnect response to Nintendo's Wii; or Zara's fashion turnover, thanks to its efficient and flexible supply chain, may come to mind. These are great examples of adapting.

But there is a difference between adapting and becoming adaptable. When organizations face a significant challenge, the business press likes to portray heroic figures galvanizing the troops to tackle "the big threat," bringing out big, bold, new ideas by tapping into the creativity of "our most valuable asset," getting these ideas prioritized through "jam sessions," and leading the company from the brink of disaster to triumphant success.

Given its recent difficulties, Nokia appears perfectly cast as the subject of just such a story. On the other hand, Nokia has been quietly adapting for almost 150 years and was an industry performance leader through the period of our research. Nokia possesses the agility factor not only because they adapt, but because they are adaptable. All long-lived organizations face existential crises when the environment turns against them. Agile organizations face them less often because they make well-considered incremental adjustments.

Thrashers also adapt, but they are not agile. Their stories make for compelling reading in the business press as they move through the phases of success, hubris, crisis, and redemption. Their long-term ROA performance resembles a sine wave, oscillating above and below the industry mean. In fact, these one-time adaptations may sow the seeds of their own undoing as the organizational learning from the transformation becomes a source of rigidity that helps precipitate the next crisis.

There is a difference between adapting and becoming

adaptable.

Two agility routines, *strategizing* and *perceiving*, facilitate the identification of what changes to consider and how best to align them for implementation. The strategizing routine sets the context and establishes the frame for what the organization does and how it goes about doing it. The perceiving routine helps agile firms develop a very clear sense of their environment and their place in it.

The strategizing routine generates three important outputs. The first and most obvious is the strategy itself. This is a living body of work that guides the activities of members of the enterprise. The second is a process for managing, monitoring, and modifying the strategy as new opportunities arise or threats emerge. The third is an aspirational purpose or mission for the organization, beyond mere profitability, that serves to unify, inspire, and direct the behaviors of organization members. In agile firms, these outputs are consistent, mutually reinforcing, and grounded in current reality. Exhibit 3.3 describes the routine in more detail.

EXHIBIT 3.3.   *The Strategizing Routine*

Element	Definition
Developing the Strategy	Confirming the organization's identity, defining its strategic intent for today's environment, and articulating the context for change
Managing Execution of the Strategy	Deploying the strategy throughout the organization, assigning accountability, monitoring performance, encouraging people to challenge the status quo, and managing processes for the resolution of challenges and development of emergent strategies
Establishing Organizational Purpose	Developing and maintaining an aspirational purpose/ mission beyond profitability, an economic model of the business, a set of core values, and norms of behavior for members of the organization that are broadly understood

Strategizing is a dynamic routine. It does not produce dead documents from an annual ritual for presentation to the board, which are then forgotten. Nor is it the rigid formulation of long-range goals and action plans followed by slavish implementation. Rather, the top management team establishes the strategic direction of the firm and sets general boundaries about what the organization will and will not do. They are careful not to overspecify the strategy; they encourage the development of *emergent* strategies from the rest of the organization. The top management teams (TMTs) of agile companies are aware of their inability to monitor all aspects of the organization and environment on their own, as well as the selection bias inherent in most organization members. Instead, they establish a climate in which they can rely on a "broad surface area" of the organization to make them aware of strategic opportunities. As Max De Pree, former CEO of Herman Miller noted, "No one of us is as smart as all of us."

As a result, there is a great deal of interaction and feedback between the *strategizing* and *perceiving* routines. The *perceiving* routine is a major source of variation in our variation-selection-retention logic of internal change that mirrors environmental forces (see "What Is Population Ecology?" in Chapter Two). In agile organizations, a large proportion of people are in contact with the external environment. Strategy and organizational purpose color their perceptions of what is important, threatening, or opportune. The perceiving routine, coupled with processes for managing the execution of the strategy, encourages members of the organization to bring forward strategic initiatives and emergent strategies that complement the overall strategic direction of the firm.

Developing the Strategy

The strategy itself consists of an enduring *identity* that derives from the organization's culture and brand promise, and a transitory *intent* that describes how the firm will meet the demands of the environment and establish a competitive advantage now. Both components of the strategy are widely shared and well understood. The idea that strategy contains two elements, one stable and the other dynamic, is not new. Writing in 1971, Ken Andrews suggested:

> ...strategy is the pattern of decisions in a company that determines and reveals its objectives...plans...and the economic and noneconomic contribution it intends to make to its shareholders, employees, customers, and communities....The pattern resulting from a series of such decisions will probably define the central

character and image of a company.... Some aspects of such a pattern of decisions may be, in an established corporation, unchanging over long periods of time.... Other aspects of a strategy must change as or before the world changes.... The basic determinants of company character, if purposefully institutionalized, are likely to persist through and shape the nature of substantial changes in product-market choices and allocations of resources.[2]

An organization's *identity* represents the shared institutional knowledge of "who we are, what we do, and how we do it." It draws from company culture, history, lore, market image, and reputation to create the organization's character and give work meaning.[3] It describes the organization's unique attributes and capabilities that made it successful in the past and have relevance today. It carries lessons on how the organization came into being, overcame adversity, developed its blockbuster product, learned from failure, and successfully grew. It provides an enduring perspective on the firm and its place in the environment.

When Steve Elop joined Nokia in 2010, he invested time and energy in learning the company's identity. Among other things, he learned that people at Nokia believe they do well by doing good. Two longtime Nokia managers tell similar stories.

When he started, Steven (Elop) solicited feedback...what shouldn't we change, what do we need to fix, etc. One of the things he heard—do not change that we are doing good in the world. We are enhancing the quality of life for people around the world. Our pride is attached to that. We have great efforts in research and sustainability that need to continue.

It's been interesting with the new CEO. The first thing he did was an open letter/email and then opened his own section in social cast [one of the many internal social and communications networks at Nokia]. He has shared what people said to him...one thing that is constantly mentioned...please change this or that, but what constantly comes out in all of the discussions, please do not change the core of the company...We are a "good company" that wants to do well both financially and other ways. It's why many people are attached to the company.

Nokia's brand reputation ranks among the top in the world for quality, reliability, and sustainability. The company's Finnish roots provide it with such values as honesty, frugality, seriousness, and directness; there is little tolerance for "political nonsense" within Nokia. Finally, Nokia has a very can-do attitude and has been through many transitions over its 150-year history, starting as a pulp and paper business in 1865. Wrapped up in its identity is the explicit notion that Nokia has changed in the past and will have to change in the future.

Nokia's marketing tagline reflects its identity: "Connecting People." Nokia sees itself as an enabler that, through communications technology, provides ready access to other people, information, and institutions in order to improve the quality of life for all its customers. By connecting people, they do good in the world.

The agile organizations we studied have identity that is consistent with current reality. The things that people *believe* are unique and make the firm successful actually *do* make it successful. They exhibit the values and behaviors that they espouse. The differentiating capabilities they set out to implement really do exist and deliver value. Their external reputation is consistent with their view of themselves. In thrashers and underperformers, however, perception and reality often diverge. Airlines that tout their differentiating customer service but do not listen to consistent passenger feedback about their poor experiences operate in ignorance and wonder why loyalty is low.

Intent, the second component of strategy, describes how the firm plans to achieve a competitive advantage now. It is driven by the fundamental economic logic of the business and the firm's position in the market. Agile firms develop a clear strategic direction—an "umbrella" strategy, as Mintzberg described it—that is shared broadly with the organization. The expectation of the TMT is that the organization will not only execute the strategy but also enhance it as opportunities arise and threats emerge. For example, Nokia's economic logic relies on volume sales to cover the fixed costs of its vertically integrated supply chain and global distribution network. Nokia directly managed the development of its handsets, from concept to consumer marketing, and produced models for every segment globally. In 2007, that amounted to over 110 million phones.

The firm's strategic positioning in the market is defined along three dimensions.

- **Breadth** is about the size, reach, and complexity of the strategy. It includes the range of products and services offered, the number of markets served, and the range of technologies applied.

- **Aggressiveness** is about speed, frequency, and tolerance for risk. It describes the extent to which the strategy "pushes the envelope" of product, service, marketing, technology, or methods and how quickly these are implemented.

- **Differentiation** describes how the organization is better, faster, cheaper, or combinations thereof. It is about the distinguishing features of products, services, and the way the business is operated, including the organization's distinctive capabilities. It answers the question, "Why do customers buy from us?"

For example, Nokia's "develop the ecosystem" intent announced by Elop was an acknowledgment that it missed a major shift in the mobile market whereby handsets became just one node in a network of operating systems, "apps," services, the Internet, and infrastructure. Its Symbian operating system, like BlackBerry, had lost out to the Apple iOS and Google Android in the "consumerization" of smartphones since 2007. As a result, it increased its aggressiveness and risk by forging a strategic alliance with Microsoft and its Windows Phone operating system in the hope that developers would provide the apps to make them viable competitors. To compete effectively with the likes of Apple and Samsung, Nokia intended to reclaim a differentiating design advantage that had grown weak under Olli-Pekka Kallasvuo. It would also differentiate through its enhanced ecosystem. Its strategic breadth remained global, competing in all handset segments, but breadth increased as Nokia sought to engage application and service provider partners.

Finally, intent must honor identity. The "develop the ecosystem" intent fully supported the "connecting people" identity. In contrast, 3M provides a cautionary tale of when a transitory strategic intent driven from the top clashes with an organization's identity. When James McNerney was hired as CEO in 2000, 3M's revenues and profits were stagnating. From 2000 through 2004, he attempted to raise profitability quickly through operating efficiency and projects that would generate results fast. He centralized decision making, introduced Six Sigma initiatives that standardized processes, and instituted cost-control measures. Although profitability improved, innovation at 3M began to suffer, and the rate of new-product introductions slowed. There was widespread resistance to attempts to standardize a complex and essentially chaotic process. 3M's rank among America's most innovative companies began to slip. Finally, George Buckley was brought in to replace McNerney in 2005, and he launched a number of initiatives to restore 3M's innovation capabilities. He later noted, "Invention is, by its very nature, a disorderly process. You can't put a Six Sigma process into that area and say, 'Well, I'm getting behind on invention, so I'm going to schedule myself for three good ideas on Wednesday and two on Friday.' That's not how creativity works."[4] The changes that realigned 3M's strategic intent with its identity paid off in the form of new products and strong performance during the Great Recession of 2008–2009.

Managing Strategy Execution

The second output of the strategizing routine is a set of processes for managing, monitoring, and modifying the strategy. The TMT plays a critical role in ensuring that this advanced good-management practice actually executes the intended strategy and allows it to be enhanced through the perceiving routine. Enhancements may come in the form of top-down strategic initiatives or emergent strategies that bubble up from other parts of the organization. To accomplish this, the TMT must facilitate communication up, down, and across the organization and provide forums where evidence-based discussions of environmental signals can be conducted by the right people at the right level, alternative responses evaluated, and decisions made.

The TMTs of agile firms push the boundaries of good management practices to support agility. First, the strategy development process is highly participative, so that the strategy incorporates diverse perceptions. Second, the strategy is communicated broadly, deeply, and continuously. Third, TMTs regularly test to ensure that all levels of the organization understand the strategy and reflect it in goals and activities. Fourth, strategic objectives and initiatives are a regular feature of the performance management process, including incentives. The urgent is not allowed to crowd out the important. Finally, the TMT invests to make resources available to the organization for the development of emergent strategies.

In this dynamic world, strategy is a wasting asset that must be continuously refreshed if it is to remain viable.

No strategy or set of differentiating capabilities will deliver value forever. Competitors constantly jockey for advantage; technology advances and accelerates development; globalization continues to flatten everything. Regulation and deregulation pressure a variety of markets, and environmental boundaries shift or, as in computing, communications, and media, break down entirely. In this dynamic world, strategy is a wasting asset that must be continuously refreshed if it is to remain viable.

But as Michael Porter wrote in 1996, not every decision or initiative is strategic.[5] Continuous improvement has been table stakes for competitiveness since the dawn of the quality movement, and it should be part of every firm's good management practice. Reducing cycle time and cost per unit, improving quality, and raising throughput should be part of day-to-day operations. Segmenting the customer base and reducing cost-to-serve while enhancing delivered quality is not strategic. Attacking a new customer segment is strategic (*breadth*). So is launching a price war (*aggressiveness*). These and other initiatives like them must be part of the evidence-based conversations described here. TMTs base their evaluation on institutional knowledge of intent, identity, experience, and environmental requirements.

Agile firms understand the distinction between what is strategic and what is not, that a current strategy's value will decline over time, and that it must be continuously updated. They also have a clear sense of their environment and their place in it. This allows them to focus their attention on creating a series of strategic intents that provide momentary competitive advantages. In a dynamic world of turbulent environments, sustainable sources of competitive advantage are few and far between, and they are not sustained for long. As a result, agile firms continuously think about the next source of advantage by combining environmental signals with institutional knowledge that sharpens their strategic intent and improves environmental fit.

Strategic change is fraught with risk. It's no wonder so many efforts fail. Frankly, the odds are against success. Why? Because organizations must get a complex sequence of decisions and actions right for the change effort to succeed. Among these is this sequential process:

1. Did we correctly interpret the environmental signals? And

2. Did we identify the most effective response? And

3. Can we apply the right resources (people, money, time) to put the response into effect? And

4. Can we get the organization behind the response? And

5. Can we implement the response in time? And

6. Did the response deliver as intended?

Theory teaches us that the probability of overall success is the product of the probability of success at each step. If the organization is pretty good at making change happen, and has, say, a 90 percent chance of success at each step ($p = 0.9$), then the overall probability of success in the preceding process is $(0.9)^6 = 0.59$. That is hardly a certainty.

Consequently, the TMTs of agile organizations put processes, tools, and institutional knowledge in place to integrate strategizing and perceiving, improve the odds of correctly interpreting what is happening in the environment, and successfully responding. It is this investment that makes agility a dynamic capability and part of the fabric of the firm. One way Nokia does this is through its worldwide direction-setting process, called "adaptive short-term planning." This six-month planning and budgeting cycle combines market signals and strategic intent. Executives blend emergent, bottoms-up, and prioritized initiatives with top-down direction into a rolling strategy statement that they communicate throughout Nokia.

Furthermore, the risk and difficulty associated with a change in the economic logic of the business is considerably greater than that of a change to market position (breadth, aggressiveness, or differentiators). The economic logic of an organization is extremely hard to change because of the investments made in specific assets, operational practices, and, most notably, differentiating capabilities. Institutionalized patterns of behavior and their reinforcement over time lead to resistance to all but incremental changes. The "paradox of success" leads to a tendency to discount or even ignore environmental signals of technical or economic disruption that call for new responses. IBM barely survived the shift from mainframe computing enabled by the CMOS technology, much of which it had pioneered. As we saw in our opening chapter, Digital Equipment Corporation did not survive at all.

If an organization needs to change its identity, it is usually in crisis. Because identity is built up over time and reinforced through experience, it cannot be changed directly or overnight. Like organizational culture, it must be addressed from the outside in. When identity no longer conforms to operational reality, and the beliefs that people hold are an impediment to making necessary changes, management must somehow "reset" the organization. In the absence of an identity that is "change friendly," which embraces change as one source of an organization's advantage, senior management, often new senior management, must recraft the organization's purpose.

Establishing Organizational Purpose

When organizations lose their way, effective leaders redirect them in a very participative process of establishing a mission or purpose for the firm. Lou Gerstner famously said, "The last thing IBM needs right now is a vision," but Sam Palmisano recognized its importance when he became CEO in 2002. Both DaVita and Harley-Davidson launched their transformations to agility with events that established a company purpose and set of values. All of the agile organizations we studied had a documented aspirational purpose that included a set of values intended to guide behaviors. We noted a major difference between the agile high-performing companies and the thrashers that we studied: a significantly higher percentage of employees in agile companies said, unprompted, that there was such a mission and they knew what it was. When successfully embedded in the psyche of the organization, the mission and values become guideposts for the realized identity and strategic intent.

In 2008, as Nokia first began to experience competitive difficulties, Olli-Pekka Kallasvuo launched a participative process to refine the company's core values of customer satisfaction, respect, achievement, and renewal. The TMT stipulated that the revised set of values had to emerge from "the many" communicating with "the many" and reflect the "connecting people" identity. The process was both high-tech and high-touch. They employed IBM's Jamming technology to establish a global chat room. After they interviewed people in their work groups, over two thousand people participated in "World Café" discussion groups.[6] Out of this emerged four new values that pushed the existing set a step further:

- **Achieving Together**—Working at Nokia means more than just collaboration and partnership; it involves trusting, sharing, and participating in formal and informal networks.

- **Engaging You**—Reflecting the old customer satisfaction value, it encourages all stakeholders, including employees, to work on the things that Nokia stands for in the world.

- **Passion for Innovation**—Nokia employees want to live their dreams, to find their courage, and to move into the future through technology and innovation that contributes to the world around us.

- **Very Human**—What the organization offers customers, how it does business, how its employees work together, and the impact of its actions and behavior on people and the environment. In short, Nokia wants to act like a very human company.

Nokia's mission is as direct as it is difficult: "Nokia's mission is simple: Connecting People. Our goal is to build great mobile products that enable billions of people worldwide to enjoy more of what life has to offer." It aligns with the current identity and establishes a goal for strategic intent. The last sentence in the mission statement, "Our challenge is to achieve this in an increasingly dynamic and competitive environment," clearly sets the context for change and alerts everyone at Nokia that nothing stays the same for long.

THE PERCEIVING ROUTINE

Agile organizations understand the power of market forces. They adopt a more humble and learning-oriented stance: "The environment will teach you if you let it."[7] Agile organizations use the perceiving routine to assess what is happening in their environment better, faster, and more reliably then their competitors. In combination with the processes of the strategizing routine, agile organizations figure out how to adapt. Researchers call this "absorptive capacity"—the ability to acquire or assimilate information and ultimately exploit it.[8] Our data, especially the data from the interviews, suggests that organizations don't do this particularly well at the scale and quality required to support agility. In many cases, the perceiving routine was only loosely connected with TMT activity. An executive from one of the thrashers in our sample put it this way: "We don't spend enough time on the future and how we want to get there. We have the data—in fact, we have a well-respected scenario process and a long-range strategic planning process—but most of the dialogue at the top is about the 'now' issues." In addition, many firms did a poor job of encouraging people to "speak truth to power." The TMTs in agile organizations see it as their responsibility to engage in ongoing, evidence-based debates that improve the quality of their interpretations of environmental signals. The effectiveness of these future-oriented senior management conversations was supported by a set of practices that encourage naysayers, positive deviants, and rabble-rousers to challenge the status quo.

The environment will teach you if you let it.

The perceiving routine gathers, analyzes, transmits, and supports the interpretation of environmental information. In broad terms, environmental data informs decisions about what a "better fit" might look like in the current environment or how the organization should make adjustments to its strategic intent, capabilities, or organization design. Environmental data also inform decisions about possible future demands so that the strategy, identity, and purpose can filter, guide, and generate alternative possible strategic intents for the future (the primary job of the testing routine). Whereas the strategizing routine develops and shapes strategies and manages the expectations regarding change and implementation, the perceiving routine is about identifying trends and changes in the many dimensions of the environment, transmitting this information to decision makers for interpretation, and formulating possible responses. The strategizing routine has an analytical and rationalizing feel, whereas the perceiving routine has a contentious, enthusiastic, and contagious feel. Our data suggest that perceiving may be the most difficult routine to build because it is more than scenario planning; it requires people in the organization to speak up, give voice, and challenge the status quo with data and information gathered from the environment.

A weak perceiving routine hamstrings the organization's ability to sense the relevance of emerging technologies, the impact of market changes, the significance of competitor announcements, or the import of political shifts. The organization is less likely to see the need for change over time because it will not be aware of the significance of signals that would otherwise change its expectations.[9] This is a common condition among thrashers, who tend to be more shortsighted than agile organizations. Their intense focus on maximizing a current advantage prevents them from seeing the signals that would suggest a change. Alternatively, if they are trying to dig out of a performance slump and are successful, they are reinforced for thinking locally. Thrashers lack the patience and rigor necessary to nurture a strong perceiving routine.

The perceiving routine has three critical features (see Exhibit 3.4). These features are partly a reflection of the organization's identity and

EXHIBIT 3.4. *The Perceiving Routine*

Element	Definition
Sensing the Environment	Continuous monitoring of all aspects of the environment by a large number of people in the organization.
Communicating Information to Decision Makers	Rapid, objective communication of information from the environment to relevant decision makers. Information flows freely and easily up and down the organization.
Interpreting Environmental Signals	Analyzing, evaluating, and interpreting information from the environment in light of the organization's strategic identity and intent, and formulating responses appropriate for its risk tolerance.

purpose and the way the TMT manages strategic expectations. Identity, purpose, and expectations send signals about the kind of initiatives that are likely to have adaptive value for the current strategic intent and how to behave, in particular about how people are expected to gather and report information and about the right communication approach. But it also reflects an awareness that these same expectations color people's perceptions. The perceiving routine includes processes to support inputs from diverse and even contrary orientations.

First, the organization must be able to sense easily what is happening in the environment. A good perceiving routine gathers a broad range of information—from current conditions and extremely likely events to alternative futures and highly improbable possibilities. Agile organizations use structure to put people in touch with different parts of the market and environment. Second, collected information must be communicated vertically and horizontally. The routine assembles that information and communicates it to the right people at the right time. Decision makers must have accurate, not sanitized or overly aggregated, findings and conclusions. Finally, the organization must be able to sort out and make sense of the data. This interpretation process—aided by scenarios and strategy—allows TMTs to formulate responses, sponsor experiments, and revise strategy. The more the identity supports open dialogue, debate, and evidence-based problem solving over political games, power grabbing, and empire building, the more effective the perceiving routine will be in preventing lock-in on a particular strategy or organization design. All three elements of perceiving environmental change are essential.

The Nokia story is interesting for the number of times the business and research press have praised or criticized the organization for its market perceptions. When it correctly senses and interprets where the market is headed, it's on the cover of business magazines for its brilliance; when it misreads the market, Nokia is on the cover for its bungling. Investors' short-term demands for returns and the business press's search for juicy headlines often miss the key point: Nokia is very active and has a number of practices in place to inquire about an unknowable future (just do a Nokia search on YouTube.com). They are very transparent—even with the media—about their thinking; they move a lot of information up, down, and through their network; and they are organized to do all of this very well. They are not always right (who is?), but their history of change and performance suggest an ability to bounce back and be right more often than they are wrong.

Sensing Environmental Change

Perceiving begins with sensing. At the heart of an organization's ability to generate new ideas, new approaches, new products, or other meaningful variations is an ability to sense how environmental demands are changing. It is facilitated by, more than anything else, the organization's structure. New strategic initiatives can come from anywhere but are most likely to come from people who have a direct connection with some aspect of the external environment.[10] Agile organizations have a way of thinking about structure that focuses attention and resources on current operations and future business opportunities. As well, the structure places as many people as possible in contact with the environment.

At the core of these structural choices is an investment dilemma: how many resources should focus on exploiting existing capabilities in service of the current strategic intent, and how many resources should focus on exploring the capabilities, businesses, and technologies that may be required for the future.[11] That is the essence of what's known as "ambidexterity"—finding the right balance between, or the right sequences of, efforts to gather information to help with current performance and efforts to learn about the future. Agile organizations create ambidextrous structures to guide organization members in thinking about the type of information to be sensed, communicated, and interpreted.

While ambidexterity helps the organization distinguish between current and future types of activities and information gathering, putting as many people as possible into direct contact with the environment increases the structure's "surface area" and the external focus of organization members. Maximizing the structure's surface area is about defining different roles in the organization with responsibility for finding out what specific stakeholders—such as customers, competitors, suppliers, regulatory agencies, market analysts, technical organizations, or nongovernmental organizations—are thinking, as well as understanding broader issues related to globalization, industry evolution, social dynamics, or political risks. Flatter structures and more differentiated roles focus people on gathering intelligence directly from different stakeholders or general environmental trends through multiple touch points, activity descriptions, and practices.

Increasing the surface area also extends to individual units and the extent to which individual and team activities explicitly include contact and information gathering from different dimensions of the environment. Because different units in different parts of the organization may gather critical information, the idea of maximizing surface area must also include exchanges of information with other internal units. Ultimately, the quality of the firm's perceiving routine depends on the roles at the interface between the firm and its environment and at the interface between subunits within the firm and the processes they use.[12]

Nokia's core organization design scores high on both ambidexterity and surface area. Nokians routinely describe the organization as very networked, highly global, highly matrixed, and quite informal and collaborative. One of the most often used adjectives is "flat." The current-future tension of ambidexterity is resolved nicely at Nokia by a strong research organization focused on the future that is separated from but integrated with the markets and devices organizations. At the same time, each organization unit faces a different dimension of the environment and contributes to the structure's overall surface area. All organization members are encouraged to stay close to stakeholders.

The Nokia Research Center (NRC) has the mandate of leading the organization into the future as "the global leader of open innovation for the human mobility systems of the fused physical and digital world, giving birth to the growth of businesses for Nokia." Created in 1986, the center has evolved to the point that its current mission is "exploring new frontiers for mobility and solving scientific challenges in order for Nokia to deliver irresistible mobile experiences in the future." The NRC's mandate goes well beyond any current business model to intentionally disrupt the status quo. The head of Nokia's research organization noted: "NRC is an extraordinary organization. We are partly aligned to the corporation and partly intentionally misaligned. We are aware of the corporate-level goals, but we are also looking at things that are not part of the current situation. It's my duty to push investment in longer-term issues and innovation. That's our purpose."

In addition, the NRC participates in "open innovation"; it is in direct contact with a variety of partner universities and think tanks and recognizes that important resources, information, and work exist outside the boundaries of the NRC.[13] To maintain this focus on the future, to ensure that the urgent work of making money today doesn't cannibalize the important work of creating opportunities for the future and the R&D organization is not funded by the product groups. The front-end, "concepting" R&D budget is 100 percent corporate funded.

The markets organization, however, is close to customers and distributors and uses environmental information to support fast and efficient execution. They gather information on how people are using the products, understanding local conditions, and how to improve current campaigns and sales. For example, when large consumer electronics retailers in India declined to carry mobile phones because of their low margins, the local Nokia markets organization—a mix of native Indians and other experts from Finland, China, and Indonesia—collaborated in listening to and observing people in various parts of India to understand their needs. Nokia and its business partner, ATL, hit on the idea of a different kind of distribution network and ran an experiment (see Chapter Four). Nokia and ATL copied the small fruit and vegetable kiosks found in villages across India and recruited individuals interested in running their own kiosks, trained them, and ensured they would have products in the right quantities and at the right margins for those vendors to make a living. The Nokia team wanted to be sure that whatever arrangement they designed would benefit Nokia, ATL, and the individual mobile phone vendors.

The mobile phone and smartphone business units face a different environment. They use medium-term information to support product design and innovation. These business groups innovate and improve on phones for respectively different markets, but their surface area extends to coordinating with each other. The mobile phone group tries to make and distribute, as widely as possible, devices with features that were innovated previously in the solutions organization. For example, a 12-megapixel camera initially offered in a smartphone can become a standard feature in the mobile phone of the future. They both drive near-term changes in breadth, aggressiveness, and differentiation with data from the environment.

Sensing Without Communicating Is Waste

Ambidextrous and broad surface-area structures put people in touch with different parts of the environment and commission them to find out what's going on. However, the quality of the perceiving routine does not simply depend on the organization's direct interface with the external environment. It also depends on transfers of knowledge across and within subunits that may be far away from the original source. The organization has to communicate and interpret that information through transparent vertical and horizontal channels so that it gets to the right people to take effective action.

At Nokia, the adaptive short-term planning process described in the strategy routine serves a second important and integrative purpose. The bottoms-up cycle is initiated by brainstorming sessions about what Nokia's priorities should be and provides a systematic forum to consider all the ideas and information being gathered by the ambidextrous, flat structure. After integration with top managers' own discussions regarding the future, the rolling strategy statement cycles back. Significantly, managers still have the autonomy to find extra money to support promising ideas that emerge.

The organization has to communicate and interpret that information through transparent vertical and horizontal channels so that it gets to the right people to take effective action.

In addition to formal processes of communication, agile organizations possess norms of proactive and transparent communication. A variety of authors—including Warren Bennis, Jim O'Toole, Robert Burgelman, and Michael Beer—have argued that the ability to foster and reinforce a climate of openness and challenge is key to the effectiveness of the perceiving routine.[14] As Burgelman put it, "An atmosphere in which strategic ideas can be freely championed and fully contested by anyone with relevant information or insight may be a key factor in developing internal selection processes that maximize the probability of generating viable organizational strategies."[15]

Although Nokia has made a number of changes in their organization structure over the years, they have never strayed very far from a very simple portrayal because so much of the work is carried on by informal social networks. (Exhibit 3.5 traces several of the more important changes.) Nokia has invested heavily in communications for well over ten years. As one executive put it, "We are always trying to look for the right balance of continuity and nimbleness. When things are in constant flux and evolution, it results in a lot of reshuffling, and the organization has learned to adapt quickly. The networked nature of the structure and communication actually helps that happen without too much disruption."

People are well connected within the company, and the connections support the way they communicate. For example, Nokia has its own internal "YouTube," a SocialCast system (a "halfway house between Facebook and Twitter"), blogs, and a variety of other formal and informal communication pathways. "We need to get things going without having to rely on meetings, and so there is a very active blogosphere that supports a combination of technologically savvy and open communications culture."

Primary Divisions	
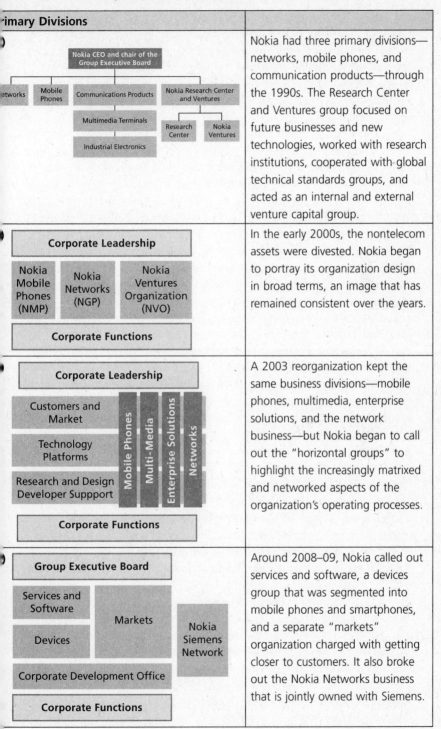	Nokia had three primary divisions—networks, mobile phones, and communication products—through the 1990s. The Research Center and Ventures group focused on future businesses and new technologies, worked with research institutions, cooperated with global technical standards groups, and acted as an internal and external venture capital group.
	In the early 2000s, the nontelecom assets were divested. Nokia began to portray its organization design in broad terms, an image that has remained consistent over the years.
	A 2003 reorganization kept the same business divisions—mobile phones, multimedia, enterprise solutions, and the network business—but Nokia began to call out the "horizontal groups" to highlight the increasingly matrixed and networked aspects of the organization's operating processes.
	Around 2008–09, Nokia called out services and software, a devices group that was segmented into mobile phones and smartphones, and a separate "markets" organization charged with getting closer to customers. It also broke out the Nokia Networks business that is jointly owned with Siemens.

Elop is a fan of the SocialCast platform. When he first came on board, he used it to ask his initial questions: "What things should I change? What things should stay the same? And what issues might I miss as I get to know the company?" He also commented on others' updates and wrote a blog giving employees more insights into the latest announcements.

Even more important, the organization expects people to engage in the debates about current and future operations, products, and initiatives. For example, Nokia set up an intranet soapbox known as Blog-Hub, opening it to employee bloggers around the world. Using aliases such as the Hulk and the Needle, organization members can be brutally critical of Nokia on issues ranging from purchasing practices to the speed of mobile-phone software. Rather than shutting them down, Nokia managers embrace the practice and credit Nokia's growth to a history of encouraging employees to say whatever is on their minds, with faith that smarter ideas will result. As one long-term executive put it, "Our role is to keep the skids greased."[16]

Creating and managing processes such as adaptive short-term planning and encouraging debate and communication are in keeping with the TMT responsibilities described in the strategizing routine. These represent opportunities for hearing about the results of debates concerning what's happening in the environment and for multistakeholder, evidence-based decision making. Agile organizations do not leave these kinds of processes to chance; rather, they design forums for debate and ensure that performance management practices recognize an individual's contribution to the process so that communicating is a way of life. For thrashers and underperformers, establishing open channels of communication, especially between the top and the bottom of the organization, can get twisted in a variety of ways. In response to a question about "bottoms-up" communication, one executive at a thrasher organization said, "Sure, everyone has my email and can send a message anytime." When asked about how those messages get aggregated and used, there was silence and note taking. More commonly, the communication process breaks down through norms such as "no bad news" or "shoot the messenger," which discourage people from raising issues and awareness with data.

The two key outputs from the communicating process are findings or conclusions and scenarios. First, the communicating process delivers findings and conclusions to decision makers through the various types of formal and informal channels just described. This process cannot deliver raw and non-aggregated data, lest the TMT be overwhelmed. Instead, the communication process adds value to the raw data and perceptions by looking for patterns that translate data into information. Moreover, data and information need to be viewed through the lens of identity, intent, and purpose as well as institutional knowledge and experience. The artful practice here is not to overly aggregate, sanitize, or get so far away from the data that decision makers lose a feel for its intensity or miss the opportunity to see how one piece of data originating in one part of the organization might connect with a similar piece of data coming from elsewhere.

Second, the communicating process is constantly delivering a revised portfolio of future scenarios. Scenarios are stories about the future, and their development is an important part of the perceiving routine (see "The History and Development of Scenarios"). Scenarios include assumptions about future events and the likely reactions of different stakeholders. Rather than trying to predict the future, creating scenarios is an opportunity to use perceptions, trends, and information to create implications about the future.[17] Obviously, the scenarios need to be developed in the first place, and they represent an important investment in the organization's agile capability. However, once they are constructed, their continued use means updating and revising them based on new information, events, and decisions.

At Nokia, the scenario development process is clearly within the purview of the NRC. An NRC senior researcher explained:

> In a very fast-changing landscape, there are some organizations that are seemingly able to do well without longer-term R&D. I say "seemingly" on purpose, because I don't believe it's true. There's a more complex answer. It depends on how fragile you believe the future is; how much uncertainty is in the landscape. The higher the uncertainty, the more you need to hedge. NRC gives the company alternatives for the future because the communications capacities and networking trends are so dynamic and uncertain. We give Nokia options.

The NRC explores disruptive technologies and future scenarios that will become the basis of strategic intents ten to fifteen years (or longer) from now. It seeks out information, trends, and possibilities; it brings in alternative scenarios, options, opinions, and forecasts. One such process conducted several years ago was called the Nokia Open Studio experiments. The program was intended to explore "opportunities for new products, applications, [and] services that would be viable within a three- to fifteen-year timeframe...*not* to generate concepts to be fed into the design process." In particular, the project wanted to understand

THE HISTORY AND DEVELOPMENT OF SCENARIOS

In October 1973, in response to the U.S. decision to resupply the Israeli armed forces during the Yom Kippur war, OPEC suspended oil shipments to the United States. Within weeks, the price of oil jumped from $3 per barrel to $12 per barrel. As these events unfolded, managers at Royal Dutch Shell decided to lower their refining investments in the Middle East and shift those investments to other parts of the value chain. As a result, Shell did not suffer from the industry's subsequent overcapacity in refining and significantly outperformed its peers. Shell's timely and quick response to the 1973 oil crisis was an important contributor to its movement from one of the weakest of the "seven sisters" to the second largest and most profitable.

From the outside, Shell's response looked nimble and brilliant. But such a view would be incomplete. A better interpretation is that they were reaping the benefits of one of the best-known examples of long-term scenario planning. Their strategic conversations about "What would we do if the unthinkable happened?" prepared them well for when the unimaginable occurred.

Scenario planning has a long history. Like many innovations, it was developed in the military for use in war games. The name most often associated with the development of scenario-based planning is that of Herman Kahn, first at the RAND Corporation, then at the Hudson Institute, which he founded after resigning from RAND. Kahn adopted the term *scenario* from Hollywood as the detailed outline of a future fictional movie. Scenarios were not predictions, but stories to be explored. Stanley Kubrick's 1964 movie character Dr. Strangelove was believed to be based on a combination of Herman Kahn and Edward Teller, the father of the H-bomb.

Early scenario-based plans replaced a single forecast of some variable with a probabilistic assessment of alternative futures. For all the additional work, there was little improvement in predictability. Consequently, this approach was abandoned in favor of one that built scenarios based on causation. The critical task of the scenario planner is to separate what is predictable from what is uncertain (that is, not subject to a probabilistic estimate). For example, in the 1973 OPEC example above, global demand for oil was relatively predictable (growing around 6 percent per year), whereas the willingness of OPEC suppliers to sell oil at prevailing prices was fundamentally uncertain.

As with any tool, there is little value in having scenarios if they are not used to drive robust strategic conversations about how the organization might respond should a situation arise. Over time, Royal Dutch Shell (RDS) realized five sources of value from scenarios:

- Better decision making around project selection and funding, as projects were required to deliver hurdle rates under a variety of alternative scenarios

- Better-quality thinking about the future, more flexible mental models, recognition of when a scenario was playing out, and an ability to take fast action

- Managerial ability to be more perceptive, to recognize patterns from the scenarios as they occurred in the real world, and to appreciate their implications

- Changing the context of decision making throughout the organization to take scenarios into account before allocating resources

- Providing strategic leadership to the organization

This last point became particularly important in the late 1980s when strategic scenarios suggested that environmental issues would become increasingly important and that responsible environmental stewardship would be important for corporate survival.

For all their investment, it was not clear that scenario planning delivered strategic differentiation or economic benefit to Royal Dutch Shell. An audit conducted in the 1980s by a team led by Arie de Geus, head of Shell's Strategic Planning Group, found that the decision-making processes following scenario development were more responsible for the lack of implementation than the scenarios themselves. Despite their power and usefulness as a vehicle to change the way managers think, scenarios still require good decisions and implementation to deliver organizational value.

the implications of a "digital divide" wherein some countries enjoy a variety of technologies while others have little access.

In 2007, the Open Studio project established "design studios"—small storefronts in local communities in India, Brazil, and Ghana—and sponsored a design contest. People from these mostly impoverished neighborhoods were given access to designers and encouraged to think about their ideal phone. "What does it look like? What does it do? How will you use it? When and where will you use it?"

The Nokia Open Studio project demonstrated one way that Nokia gains insight into how developing markets are thinking about the use of technology and how its technology should adapt in the future. In addition, the process of collecting information about the future generated a range of positive social benefits. Local people were hired to run the studios, and the studios became a place for people to convene. That was an immediate benefit for the community but also built long-term good-will. The project generated data about the use of technology and how technology might get diffused.

Communicating Without Interpreting Is Noise

The final process in the perceiving routine, interpreting, completes the circle between strategizing and perceiving. Agile organizations need to have some standards against which to judge the relevance of a piece of information, and the standards are current strategy (identity and intent), purpose, and scenarios of the future (including their assumptions). When findings and conclusions are communicated, these standards form the context for looking at the data, trying to make sense of it, and determining courses of action. The result of interpretation—another open debate—can range from initiatives to fundamentally change the organization's purpose and identity, to recognition of the need for a new business model, strategic intent, or set of differentiating capabilities, to adjustments in positioning or minor changes in operations. Many outputs of the perceiving routine become inputs to the testing and implementing routines.

A TMT is likely to spend most of its interpreting discussions on how environmental change will affect the current strategic intent and what, if anything, should be done. It is a problem-solving conversation that most executives are familiar with. However, a TMT must be open to broader and more radical implications. Findings and conclusions that challenge the existing economic logic, identity, or mission are especially hard to hear if they signal the need for change that is more fundamental than relatively straightforward adjustments to breadth, aggressiveness, and differentiation. We know from psychology that there is a bias to dismiss such data even though they may be right. TMTs must possess the methods and group dynamics to challenge their own assumptions or have a process in place for having others, such as a board of directors, who can challenge assumptions. Either way, having a culture in which the status quo can be challenged is important.

When an organization needs to have broader discussions, one effective way to work through the interpreting process is to employ alternative scenarios. TMTs in agile organizations spend a lot of time understanding a portfolio of scenarios, their assumptions, and the nuances of their implications. As we saw in the DaVita case, the senior leaders engage in lengthy debates about health care reform, how legis-lation and social trends will affect it, and how it might evolve. An important outcome of these discussions is a set of responses the organization might make and decision options under the "What would we do if this were true?" contingency. For each scenario, there is one or more sets of designed responses that the organization could put into effect.

As new data come in, the scenarios and their assumptions are discussed:

- Are any of these scenarios more probable?

- Do any of the data we are receiving confirm or contradict the assumptions underneath these scenarios?

- Do any of the scenarios and their response/decision portfolios seem probable enough to warrant resource allocation decisions or the initiation of experiments or initiatives?

- How should our assumptions and the scenarios be revised to reflect new beliefs or understandings?

Understanding the implications of scenarios and making informed judgments about environmental data require deep expertise about the issues. Deep expertise can come from internal experiences and learning or from external resources, such as subject matter experts, consultants, futurists, and others. However, research suggests that internal expertise is more valuable for the perceiving process because of its intimate connection with identity and purpose.[18]

Agile organizations rely on their perceiving routine and its open, challenging climate to distinguish important signals from mere noise. Their ambidextrous structures and direct environmental contact, along with shared understanding of strategy and purpose, combine to create a wellspring of organizational knowledge and an exposure to all that is going on. Expertise allows the organization to better understand and evaluate early data about technology, market trends, or other variables. In uncertain environments, this ability allows a firm to ascertain more accurately the relevance of particular information. Thus organizations with more sophisticated perceiving routines will tend to be more proactive, exploiting opportunities in the environment independent of current performance. In addition, research suggests that maintaining alignment with environmental demands is partly a function of the organization's ability to identify and respond to environmental signals well before their performance implications are known.[19]

Our description of the perceiving routine, and especially the interpretation process, assumes the TMT has prioritized the activities related to creating a climate of debate and trust, managing execution of the strategy, and seeing the value of tightly integrating perceiving with strategizing. Establishing ambidextrous and flat structures, creating processes of communication, and using scenarios to sort out environmental signals is critical for sound strategic decision making. Thrashers and underperformers, with inward-looking and politicized managements, find this level and intensity of communication congenitally difficult. They are too busy vying for turf, resources, and position to consider dispassionately the implications of outside signals. The external focus of agile companies enables them to face up to brutal facts and separate wheat from chaff.

Thrashers and underperformers, with inward-looking and politicized managements, find this level and intensity of communication congenitally difficult.

CONCLUSION

Between 1865 and 2009, Nokia repeatedly made changes in its strategic intent that aligned the organization to its environment, and between 1984 and 2009, it made important adjustments that aligned the organization to the telecommunications industry. It wasn't always on the leading edge of technology, but its products better fit what the market wanted at the time, whether it was phones that were easy to use, had a cool user interface, could change ringtones, or had the right look and feel. Its supply chain was also generally able to get the right phones, in the right quantities, at the right costs, at the right times out to retailers and cellular operators. There was something about the way Nokia worked that made it more pragmatic, more focused, and more flexible than other companies.

As shown in Exhibit 3.6, Nokia's agility scores were all above average. Strategizing and testing were moderately above average, whereas perceiving and implementing were slightly above average.

Nokia's future will be determined by a combination of what happens in its environment and how it chooses to respond. In 2013, Nokia lost the global market share lead, and its two primary competitors, Apple and Samsung, aggressively pushed their advantage. Market share has always been a critical element in Nokia's economic logic, and they were hurt by their unwillingness in the mid-2000s to bend to the structure

EXHIBIT 3.6.   *Nokia's Agility Scores*[20]

	Strategizing	Perceiving	Testing	Implementing
Nokia	Moderately Above Average	Slightly Above Average	Moderately Above Average	Slightly Above Average

and dynamics of the North American market. Selling their mobile devices business to Microsoft, an organization to which they hitched their star in 2011 to build the third ecosystem, represented an acknowledgment that they had slipped. But Nokia has faced challenges before, and, as we have tried to demonstrate in this chapter, it still has the routines that have helped them in the past and will help them in the future.

CHAPTER

4

TESTING AND IMPLEMENTING

It is not always what we know or analyzed
before we make a decision that makes it a
great decision. It is what we do after we make
the decision to implement and execute it
that makes it a good decision.

—WILLIAM POLLARD

Rich Fairbank and Nigel Morris founded Capital One in 1994 believing that information technology could be used to understand consumer behavior and create niches in the credit business. Their initial analysis—that many people were carrying large credit card balances and paying interest rates in excess of 20 percent—led to an experiment. They offered a specific group of people the opportunity to transfer their balances at no cost to a new credit card with a lower interest rate. The offer struck a chord with the sample, and they extended the offer to a broader audience. It may seem like a no-brainer now, but in 1994 the balance transfer offer was a novel idea. Today, Capital One runs thousands of these—admittedly more sophisticated—experiments every year.

If you talk to anyone at Capital One long enough, you are going to hear the phrase "test and learn." The original experiment just described is no longer restricted to credit card proposals. A test can be as small as a new way of organizing or a new way of giving performance appraisals and as broad as a new product or a new line of business. It is any number of actions, decisions, or projects intended to test a hypothesis and find out if something works. Did the test generate expected results? Was it the way it was implemented or was it the idea itself? Can this be scaled up? Did it result in the kinds of benefits we wanted or wholly new benefits we never thought of?

In short, the organization implements an idea on a small scale and watches carefully what happens; it learns from the experiments. It learns from the successes as well as the failures. Over the years, for example, Capital One has learned that selling cell phones and running vacation home time-shares weren't its core competence. When a test works and it supports the organization's identity and intent, it is scaled up.

By 2000, Capital One was testing and learning a lot, and each learning implied an organization change. Successful tests in a variety of businesses meant changing skill sets, training programs, work processes, call center protocols, IT systems, regulatory compliance, and so on. The organization knew that change was never going to end and so invested in the capability to implement change.[1]

By 2003, Capital One had embedded a change capability that it used to implement large-scale systems conversions, a customer experience imperative, workplace arrangements (the "Office of the Future"), adaptations to Sarbanes-Oxley regulations, and more recently, adjustments to the Great Recession. Capital One was able to quickly hand back the TARP monies used to shore up the banking sector and passed the "stress test" on the first round. In fact, a strong perceiving routine coupled with the change capability allowed it to exit the hazardous subprime mortgages market before others. Executives attribute much of their success in managing change to the way the change capability is embedded in the line organization, not in HR or another staff function.

Capital One clearly demonstrates the two agility routines that are the focus of this chapter: testing and implementing. Testing and implementing complement the strategizing and perceiving routines to address a critical organizational dilemma: addressing the tension between allocating resources to drive current results and allocating resources to develop future products/services and businesses. All organizations must balance innovation and execution, exploration and exploitation.[2]

3M is famous for its innovation capability and in particular for its "15 percent rule," which suggests that organization members should spend 15 percent of their time thinking about new ideas. But, as the former head of R&D said, "I'll now make a confession: the 15 percent part of the 15 percent rule is essentially meaningless. Some of our technical people use much more than 15 percent of their time on projects of their own choosing. Some use less than that; some use none at all. The number is not as important as the message, which is this: the system has some slack in it. If you have a good idea, the commitment to squirrel away time to work on it, and the raw nerve to skirt your lab manager's expressed desires, then go for it."[3]

What is often lost is the implication of this rule. Embedded in the expectation that a 3M employee will spend the right amount of time innovating and trying out new ideas is the expectation that the employee will spend the right amount of time executing.[4] Spending 15 percent of your time exploring implies that you should be spending 85 percent of your time exploiting. Agile organizations are able to embed exploration and exploitation in the everyday life of organization members. Strategizing, perceiving, testing, and implementing are not discrete processes pursuing a single-minded notion of efficiency or profit maximization, but an integrated and mutually reinforcing set of routines designed to discover, develop, and implement new possibilities.[5]

Strategizing and perceiving routines provide the context and degree of freedom necessary to adapt to uncertain environments. Although new initiatives can come from anywhere, they are most likely to come from people who have deep connections to the environment and who are accountable for action.[6] Ideas are generated, small bets are placed, and risks explored. At some point, organizations need to find out which ideas are worthy and which are merely "bright shiny objects." Testing and implementing are about an organization's capacity to use the knowledge that has been collected.[7] The role of testing is to allocate resources for experimentation, to try out ideas and pilot opportunities quickly, and to learn from those trials whether or not it makes sense to invest in more substantive ways. The outputs of testing are new products, new processes, new business models, new strategies, or new businesses for implementation, the sine qua non of agility.

This chapter is focused on understanding the specifics of the testing and implementing routines and how the full weight of the innovation-execution tension is manifest in them. It also further examines how the four routines are connected with each other. We cannot begin to talk about testing and implementing without understanding that the strategizing and perceiving processes are at work generating strategic intents and a variety of information for the organization to digest. If there is no leeway to speak truth to power, no empowerment to try things out, and no freedom to innovate and test, then an organization will not generate sufficient options when the environment demands something new.

Over the course of the chapter, we will explore how a specialty retailer's ethic of experimentation and learning permeates the organization, reflecting its identity. Testing and implementation are tightly integrated with each other and with the retailer's perceiving and strategizing routines. We will also learn about the implementing routines at Netflix and how their human resource policies and change routines support agility.

TESTING IS RISK AND INNOVATION WELL MANAGED

We hear a lot about innovation these days. Under the banner of innovation, managers and employees are encouraged to ideate, rapidly prototype, and build narratives. If an organization is not pursuing disruptive, "game changing" innovation, it is most likely reacting to it.[8] Innovation is not some mystical process or outcome, nor is it as hard and intractable as most people make it out to be. Quite simply, an innovation is anything that is *new to the organization*—a new product, a new structure, a new market, or a new incentive system.

For an organization that doesn't have an enterprise resource planning program, implementing SAP is a big innovation even though the technology has been around for years. When R&D thinks of a new compound that could be commercialized quickly, it is innovating; when the Six Sigma folks identify a new source of waste, they are innovating; and when a manager thinks of a new way to motivate her people, she is innovating. Although each new idea may come from a different place, they all have one thing in common. They are trying to improve performance or effectiveness. Agility is not only about how to create new, innovative ideas; it is also about how to "test" whether those ideas can generate value.

Testing is a sophisticated routine for conceptualizing, resourcing, running, and learning from experiments (see Exhibit 4.1). It's about seeing if any of these sources of variation—new compounds, wasteful processes, or motivation techniques—actually make a difference. Perhaps most important, testing is about having a clear notion of success so that data can be generated quickly to detect errors or progress, make adjustments, and try again, or, if necessary, pull the plug on ideas that don't work. In today's parlance, it's about learning how to fail fast. Reinforced by the open and challenging climate established as part of strategizing, testing reflects an air or attitude of "Let's try it" and being convinced by evidence.

Innovation does not happen according to a schedule, but it is the result of a disciplined process. Testing is disciplined, not dogmatic; creative, not chaotic. "Eureka moments can neither be predicted nor willed a priori, but they require prior engagement—a paradox captured by Pasteur when he observed that 'chance favors only the prepared

EXHIBIT 4.1. *Elements of the Testing Routine*

Testing Routine	
Setting Up the Test	Establishing hypotheses, success criteria, schedules, resource requirements, and executive sponsorship. Failure is accepted as a legitimate test outcome and a vehicle for learning.
Running the Test	Assigning capable resources in people, time, money, and tools. Employing rigorous project management and review to maintain objectivity while enabling executive restraint.
Learning from the Test	Capturing and applying learning from the outcome of the test as well as the testing process so the organization's capabilities are continuously improved.

mind.' "[9] Testing in agile organizations requires an architecture that balances stage gates, linear road maps, schedules, and other project management techniques intended to reduce uncertainty and costs with the messy, nonlinear flow of creativity, innovation, incubation, and learning.

> *Innovation does not happen according to a schedule,*
>
> *but it is the result of a disciplined process. Testing is*
>
> *disciplined, not dogmatic; creative, not chaotic.*

Thus we chose the term *testing* instead of innovating for this routine. It highlights that innovation—like strategy—is only an idea until it is implemented and generates value that can be recognized on an income statement or seen in new behaviors.[10] The basic testing process consists of setting up the test, running experiments, and learning from the results.

THE TESTING ROUTINE AT ZIP BRANDS

Capital One isn't the only organization with a great testing routine. A specialty fashion retailer we'll call Zip Brands (not its actual name) is an organization built on a disciplined testing routine. The family business was started by a charismatic founder, Arthur, and there is no denying that the company's success is the result of his insights and learning. Arthur learned the business from the ground up, managing stores and displays, serving as the distribution manager out of his station wagon, and learning the merchant craft. As the organization grew, he recognized that doing everything himself was not only impossible but bad for the company. His first hiring decision was to add someone to take over store deliveries.

Shortly after coming to work, the new delivery guy came to Arthur and said "I can save us some money." He knew the owner of a nearby gas station who was willing to extend the fledgling start-up a discount if they agreed to buy all their gas from him. Arthur agreed, they tried it, and it worked. Later on, the same delivery man had ideas about how to make the delivery schedule more efficient. The moral of the story, told to new hires and repeated often in the company, was twofold. First, innovation is not something that lives in the business; it lives in the people who work there. Second, good ideas should be tried out to see if they work. There was, from the early years of Zip Brands, a collective curiosity to figure out how things worked, to try new things, or to see things differently, and Arthur has spent a good part of his life embedding a series of lessons learned about agility into the organization.

Testing Complements Strategizing and Perceiving

Zip Brands' testing routine complements its strategizing and perceiving routines. Its history of success has always depended on an external focus, keeping one eye on customers and one eye on markets. Zip Brands' executives talk frequently about the core competence of the organization—understanding the customer—and how this ability has matured over time. The satisfaction and pride in making a difference in people's lives is part of its culture and identity. Zip Brands sees its success as deriving from its emotional connection to its customers.

From the early 1970s to the late 1980s, understanding the customer meant serving the same customer over different life phases and recognizing that different customers want different things. Zip Brands served them through various specialty retail chains offering women's fashion, menswear, sportswear, plus sizes, adolescent lifestyle, lingerie, and personal care products. The company was highly decentralized, and each brand operated more or less independently.

In the late 1980s, aided by data from its scenario planning and strategic patterning processes, Zip Brands' executives perceived several trends in the retail market that led to another phase of the company's evolution. First, the real estate market had turned flat; future growth was unlikely to come from adding more stores. Second, the specialty retail store segment was commoditizing. Margins were shrinking, the relative amount of consumer spending on apparel had not increased, and there was no intense loyalty to one store. Finally, competition was increasing both externally and internally. Under the decentralized model, each of the individual brands competed against the others where product lines or concepts overlapped.

In this context, Arthur believed that Zip Brands needed a strategic intent that was primarily brand and margin related. Consequently, Zip Brands radically shifted its portfolio of brands and stores. Zip went from a diverse set of specialty retail chains to three overarching brands. What did not change—the organization's identity—was the importance of maintaining the emotional connection to the customer. A set of core values emerged over time to support the importance of knowing the customer well (see Exhibit 4.2).

Testing Generates Options

Coupled with the strategizing and perceiving routines in Zip Brands is a set of testing processes that generate new products, brands, and improvements. The Zip Brands testing routine employs a flexible resource allocation framework that: (1) balances the tension between innovation and execution, (2) embeds the setting up and running of experiments in the businesses, and (3) captures learnings. It all begins with a flexible view of resources.

EXHIBIT 4.2. *Zip Brands' Values*

Customers First	Everything we do must begin and end with an insatiable drive to anticipate and fulfill our customers' desires.
Aim to Win; Play Fair	Winning consistently means doing what is right—following our beliefs and the rules—when no one is watching. Winning means nothing unless how we get there is fair, collaborative, rooted in our values, and contributes to the greater good.
Enthusiasm Matters	We pursue excellence because we are emotionally, intellectually, and spiritually engaged in our work. It's what makes our talent formidable and our results extraordinary.
Be a Good Citizen	People and organizations should be well-balanced; they should do well and good, and Zip Brands has made strong and lasting commitments to being a good community citizen.

Resourcing Innovation and Execution

The traditional view is that efficiency, leanness, and cost cutting —finding and eliminating slack resources in service of today's profits— should receive top priority in management decision making. While considerable lip service is given to the importance and ease of moving new ideas around in an organization, the single-minded devotion to profitability through efficiency often means that top management and organizations are unable to appreciate the value of a novel idea they didn't create.[11] It's a naïve view in today's world because it results in an organization that may be effective now but is starving its future.

The single-minded devotion to profitability through efficiency is a naïve view in today's world because it results in an organization that may be effective now but is starving its future.

At Zip Brands, there is a healthy respect and a clear framework for managing the tension between innovation and efficiency. As one executive told us,

> This is one thing, organizationally, we are set up for. We ask the brands to focus on the sell side. That means focusing on the value to the customer, not the cost. Then we've got a really strong sourcing and logistics and design/real estate organization that really is focused on cost. So the tension is balanced in the organization's purposes.

Based on that logic, the executives understand their role vis-à-vis innovation. Two brand executives describe their perspective:

> My team is focused on the [current operational] priorities as we understand them. However, if something comes my way, I'm able to take my key creative folks and think about how to make it work. I will incubate an idea at a small and higher level, but I have to sort it out myself. We are always testing in adjacent categories. We have the freedom and expectation to try things out and to see if they work. At the [corporate] level, on the other hand, the company understands what it means to extract talent and focus them on an idea worth incubating.

> There are lots of informal touch points. This is the kind of environment where you know a lot of associates by name, know

what they do, interact with them in the cafe or walking down the hall. There are few formal lines of communication through the hierarchy, and people feel comfortable reaching multiple levels beyond their boss to discuss product ideas. We try to create opportunities to gather those ideas from anyone; we want to hear as many observations/perceptions that people have—we're all customers, all entitled to views of fashion, and just experiencing the product in a customer kind of way.

This shared view of focusing on current and future performance, efficiency and innovation, formal and informal structures, results in the flexible movement of people, resources, budgets, and ideas. One executive recognizes that she has to produce results, but not at the expense of a good idea; another executive notes how there is slack in the organization's resource base that promotes "planned spontaneity." These executives know the identity and intent of Zip Brands, they understand the values and the importance of making a connection with customers, and within that framework they have the expectation and ability to focus resources on their best and highest use. Under the value of "Aim to Win; Play Fair" and the attitude that winning must be sustainable, slack and risk taking are built into budgets.

Setting Up and Running Experiments

Agile organizations are very good at embedding the process of setting up and running experiments. They have strong commitments to testing hypotheses, creating prototypes, and listening to the market's voice. Senior executives at Zip Brands meet regularly with the brand leaders to find out "What's new? What are you seeing in your stores? How are your tests working out?" Executives ask leaders to spend about 20 to 30 percent of their time thinking about the future.

The most common story at Zip Brands is the practice of starting something small in the back of the store and watching what happens. It's a pattern that has been repeated over and over to incubate and grow new businesses. When tests are manageable in size, they do not become a distraction. Too many retailers open thirty 4,000-square-foot stores that crash and burn. Zip Brands tries something with four 500-square-foot spaces inside an existing store, sees what happens, and tracks it carefully. When the bets are too big, the risk is deemed to be too great. Arthur has a reputation for playing with an idea, working with the merchant leaders, thinking through the financial side, and then, and only then, driving it to scale. As one executive put it, "It's always the experiments and the small things that get noticed that turn out to be big things."

Running experiments applies to nonproduct ideas as well. For example, Zip Brands has experimented with putting "ready reserve talent" in the headquarters organization to support the brands in much the same way that DaVita organizes its "village scouts." However, unlike DaVita, Zip Brands learned that it was more effective to deploy talent in the brands and work with them in an invested way instead of taking on an expert role and telling the brands what to do. Similarly, an enterprise integration group created to help manage the "white space" was considered a distraction from the business and abandoned. In general, although the organization has been willing to take chances, they haven't been penny wise and pound foolish, and they know to pull the plug if something isn't working.[12]

Learning from Experiments

One of the most critical aspects of the testing routine is learning. Whereas a flexible resource allocation system balances innovation and execution, learning involves disruption and change as well as reliability and efficiency. An organization that does not capture learning from its tests—that doesn't test *and* learn—is squandering its testing resources.

First, learning is essential to codify the reasons for successful tests so that the success can be repeated. This facilitates the transfer from testing to implementing in which successful tests are scaled up. Second, learning from failed tests often forms the basis for new innovations and creates options for the future.[13] For example, capturing learning is a big part of 3M's success, and the organization deliberately records the insights from innovation attempts that don't work out. These stories become part of a technology platform, and as a technology matures, these once worthy ideas can become, again, sources of opportunity. Instead of being abandoned as mistakes or dead ends, failed tests often represent a preadaptation to an emergent future. Today's failures can become tomorrow's successes.

Zip Brands executives had similar stories. They described a concept that had been tested for a couple of years, but it was unsuccessful. Now, years later, the same idea was being tried with a slightly different merchandise assortment. It's a test, it has costs, and there are understood risks. If after a while it isn't working, they will pull the plug. Zip Brands had tried something that did not work, but the learning from that experiment was captured and, in a different time and place, was readily available. Even more interesting was that this experiment was happening in 2008, as the recession was being felt.

Learning may help explain why agile organizations appear to respond so quickly. It's not just that they perceived a trend or opportunity, marshaled resources quickly, and executed flawlessly. Rather, agile organizations invest in learning, and in different circumstances, old learning becomes new innovation.

Learning and reflection—as much as testing and innovation—are key parts of the routine. Learning is important in order to become better at running tests. There are always variables that cannot be controlled and make it difficult to isolate cause and effect. Was it the weather that caused increased sales, or the product assortment? With learning, experiments can be set up and run more efficiently and effectively. Similarly, a culture of learning allows agile organizations to be better at a lot of things, including strategizing, perceiving, and implementing. Zip Brands has been consistent in codifying its learnings, based mostly on the experiments that didn't go well the first time. Agile organizations recognize that the primary purpose of the testing routine is to validate change possibilities and to understand the potential of ideas. They also have a deep appreciation that it is the mistakes and the trials and the story telling—the learning—that allows an organization to adapt over the long term.

The testing routine is an important part of Zip Brands' agility profile (see Exhibit 4.3). It complements the other routines, all of which are moderately above average. The importance of testing is not only that it validates an idea, project, business, or product; testing integrates information collected in the perceiving process and connects it to activities in the implementation process. The perceiving routine—being close to the customer—complements the testing routine. Together, they take the time to know the customer well and generate learnings and stories that are passed down. Because so many tests are done in the stores, in the field under live conditions, Zip Brands has an easier time transferring successful tests to the implementation routine and scaling them up. No routine by itself is able to handle the uncertainty and complexity of

EXHIBIT 4.3.   *Zip Brands' Agility Profile*

	Strategizing	Perceiving	Testing	Implementing
Zip Brands	Moderately Above Average	Moderately Above Average	Moderately Above Average	Moderately Above Average

today's environments, but Zip Brands has strong routines that together help it to adapt better than most in a fast-paced industry.

IMPLEMENTING IS CHANGE WELL MANAGED

The testing routine explores and evaluates new products, new business models, and new businesses that may (or may not) add up to new strategic intents. Whether a new intent—and the capabilities associated with it—is implemented is partly a function of how much potential is left in the current one.[14] If the current strategy retains a lot of upside, the organization must balance the incentive to do something new with the potential of the current strategy. "Because the [current] strategy is rooted in organizational experience and learning, top managers are likely to be reluctant to make frequent changes in it."[15]

The recent situation at Microsoft is illustrative. Even though then-CEO Steve Ballmer announced that Microsoft would pursue a "devices and services" strategy and articulated why the change was important, many Microsoft managers continued to act as if it were still a software company. A similar situation at Intel thirty years earlier led Andy Grove to say, "One of the toughest challenges is to make people see that these self-evident truths are no longer true." To find the balance, organizations must have both a strong change capability and people who accept change as normal.

The strategic choices associated with continuous improvements in the current strategy or with adopting a new one imply two types of change in agile organizations: execution and implementation. In arguing that execution is the most important aspect of achieving performance, Larry Bossidy and Ram Charan were half right.[16] Execution refers to running the business, exploiting current advantages by carrying out the thousands of adjustments required to continuously improve within an existing economic logic and intent. In that respect, execution is the most important source of current performance. However, the very act of execution, focusing attention and resources on current activities, can blind an organization to environmental change and the need to adapt.

Implementation is much riskier and more complex than execution. It requires building a business, adjusting or changing all or nearly all of the organization's design features to support a new strategy or build new capability sets that may not be fully understood or owned by organization members. It involves changing the business and making the changes stick. An organization must invest in new skills and people, operational capacity, and other organizational routines to scale up new capabilities.

Execution involves doing better what you already know, understand, or have accepted; implementation involves learning to do well what you may not yet understand or are trying to do for the first time. Part of that learning involves accepting that the new way of working is the right way. The perceiving and testing routines work together with the implementing routine. Perceiving and testing help to keep one eye on the future, while the implementing routine keeps the other eye on the present.

Execution involves doing better what you already know, understand, or have accepted; implementation involves learning to do well what you may not yet understand or are trying to do for the first time.

As described in previous chapters, the top management team sets the context and manages the ambidexterity of driving current results and preparing the organization to implement new strategies. Perceiving and testing are the important routines for generating future implementation options, but the organization still must execute today. Top management must communicate a balanced interest to ensure that power does not rest in one activity. From a pragmatic, resource-sharing point of view, managers must structure resource flows between the two activities.[17] Implementation and execution cannot be independent activities. They must share resources, history, and experience. On the other hand, if they are overly integrated, the lure of profit today will kill the creativity of changing for profit tomorrow.

Executing and implementing both rely on the ability to change and verify that those changes made a difference in intended ways (see Exhibit 4.4). Thus, it is critical that organizations support change and put in place reviews of the implementation and effectiveness of key changes.

THE IMPLEMENTING ROUTINE AT NETFLIX

Few companies had the agility to make it through the dot-com bubble, let alone to thrive in the rapidly changing technology world that has followed it. Netflix is one company that did. It developed and implemented a variety of new strategies and capabilities since its formation in 1997 and going public in 2000. Its first business was the distribution of rented DVDs by mail, and Blockbuster was its major competitor.

EXHIBIT 4.4.   *The Implementing Routine*

Element	Description
Managing Implementation of the Change	Providing managers with autonomy, accountability, meaningful incentives, and embedded change capability so that implementation proceeds with speed, certainty, and precision.
Ensuring Delivery of Expected Results	Running postmortem reviews that check outcomes against anticipated results, identifying sources of variance, capturing the learning from successes and failures, and continuously refreshing the organization's knowledge base.

Blockbuster controlled 38 to 40 percent of the video rental market in 2002 and sold and rented DVDs through a U.S. network of over four thousand stores.[18]

Blockbuster offered convenience. Stores were a short drive away in nearly every major residential neighborhood, and its low rental prices for VHS tapes and then DVDs were attractive. The convenience strategy implied that Blockbuster's business model depended on movie turnover. When it came to new releases, renting new DVDs multiple times over a short period was the key to their making a profit. Blockbuster offset their low rental price and supported the business model by requiring customers to return the movie quickly—often within twenty-four hours from the time of rental. If you missed the deadline, late fees were assessed. Some customers wound up owing Blockbuster more than it cost to buy the movie.

Netflix disrupted the video rental industry with a different economic logic. After signing up for a monthly subscription, customers maintained a queue of their favorite movies on the Netflix website. DVDs came in the mail, often the next day, and included a postage-paid envelope to return them. Customers could keep up to five DVDs (depending on their chosen plan) at home for as long as they wanted, and when they returned one, another showed up. Their digital rights agreements and distribution system capabilities allowed Netflix to support a broad range of content—including movies, TV shows, video games, concerts, and documentaries—that was not dependent on a title's turnover.

But Netflix was not a one-trick pony. Technology and digital content continued to evolve, and Netflix recognized that to survive and thrive in a hypercompetitive environment, its business model had to evolve as well. In 2007, it started the streaming business, whereby customers could log on and simply watch the movie online, alongside the DVD-by-mail business. And then it hit a rough patch.

Netflix and its streaming business were in the press a lot during the third quarter of 2011, and it was not the kind of press they wanted.

"New Netflix Pricing Gets Thumbs Down" (*Wall Street Journal*, September 16, 2011)

"Netflix's Qwikster Announcement Leaves Subscribers Angry and Analysts Cold" (Reuters, September 19, 2011)

Analysts and customers criticized Netflix for its handling of a price increase and service change. It started, innocently enough, with a price increase in July 2011. Netflix noted that its two services—DVD home delivery and video streaming—had different business models that required different pricing approaches. Whereas customers had previously paid one low price for both DVDs by mail and streaming, going forward there would be two prices: a low price for DVDs by mail and a low price for streaming. For those who wanted to retain both, it represented a price increase of 60 percent.

By September 2011, the overwhelmingly negative reaction to the new pricing compelled CEO Reed Hastings to apologize in a blog post for the way the pricing announcement was handled. However, in the same post, he also announced that a new and independent subsidiary called Qwikster would take over the DVD delivery business while Netflix would focus on the streaming business. If the price change announcement had been awkward, the Qwikster announcement was downright clumsy.

Netflix had added insult to injury. In trying to create a challenging work environment where managers and organization members owned their own business, it overlooked customer concerns that dealing with two subscriptions, two websites, two credit card entries, and two service agreements was inconvenient. Managing two different but complicated, highly technical, ruthlessly competitive, and fast-growing businesses should not be the customer's problem.

The day after Netflix revealed that it had lost eight hundred thousand U.S. subscribers and projected far slower growth for the rest of the year, its stock price dropped 35 percent, down a total of 74 percent (or $11.6 billion in market cap) from its July 2011 high. On October

10, 2011, Hastings reversed the Qwikster decision and acknowledged that separating the two businesses had been the wrong move.

The price increase and business restructure decisions Netflix made had not been properly tested. They may have passed the appropriate internal hurdles, but they failed the final and most important one—customer acceptance. Although it was a brutal three-month period for Netflix, in keeping with the spirit of the testing routine, Netflix learned some hard but important lessons. A Netflix executive observed,

> We do things differently today because of that experience, and they're meaningful, important things. For example, you don't want to have a big heavy-duty process around small decisions. But for big decisions, we found that we needed a different process that allows for alternative opinions to have time to take root and be developed and be argued and debated.

Although during this episode predictions of Netflix's demise were common, anyone who doubted Netflix's continued success underestimated its ability to change. Agile organizations, as we saw in Chapter Three with Nokia, are not perfect, but they do have the ability to change, including the ability to recover. Since 2011, Netflix has expanded internationally, moved into content development (and won Emmys for its series *House of Cards*), and is building out its own content distribution network (Open Connect). In December 2013, Netflix passed HBO in subscribers, its stock price was near an all-time high, and it was very profitable. To say it has come a long way from DVD home delivery and competing with Blockbuster is an understatement. It has repeatedly transformed itself as the business and technology environment has changed.

The ability of Netflix to implement major changes in its business model (and to recover from missteps) is a convincing demonstration of Netflix's agility. It is able to change because:

- It has a clear and shared view about how to manage its human capital in support of agility.

- It views leadership as a capacity in the organization that needs to be developed.

- It has the capability to make major and minor organization and strategy changes; it knows how to execute and implement.

Talent Management and Leadership at Netflix

As described in Exhibit 4.4, the implementing routine involves the ability to change and to determine if the changes worked. Implementation depends vitally on the way the organization leads its people and measures the effectiveness of its changes. Netflix has outstanding credentials in this regard. They have a rigorous and clear view of their talent and performance management policies and practices (see the sidebar "Travel Light"). They make implementing and executing a normal and integrated part of the business.

TRAVEL LIGHT

Kodak's shift from chemical to digital imaging was a long, painful, and ultimately unsuccessful one. Everyone knew what had to be done: Kodak had to build new capabilities to operate a radically different technology and business model. Their initial attempts to work within the existing organization and with existing talent resources were resisted and ineffective. Ultimately, Kodak's decision to not retrain its chemical engineers but to go into the market, to hire new engineers steeped in the new technology, and to acquire companies that had the competencies it needed proved much more effective, but it was implemented too late.

For decades, talent management approaches have been built on the belief that the best way to ensure that organizations have the right people is to develop them, invest in them, and retain them in a relatively long-term employment relationship. A number of tools and processes were developed to support this career approach, including assessment centers, selection tests, career paths, behaviorally anchored rating scales, benefits management, broadbanding, competency modeling, and multiple training and development programs. Utilizing these tools required significant investments in education, certification, and experience in statistics, industrial/organizational psychology, and even finance. They were used to refine the person-job fit in organizations as well as improve execution and organizational stability. When it worked well, the career approach instilled loyalty and encouraged individuals to make sacrifices for the good of the organization. It also helped to attract and retain talented individuals. Organizations with strong development orientations, like GE, were able to pick from among the cream of the crop.

The career approach runs into trouble when the need for new skills and new approaches to dealing with business issues moves faster than they can be learned and developed. Lou Gerstner's transformation of IBM required a number of large layoffs in an organization that was admired for its lifetime, womb-to-tomb, no layoffs reputation. The mutual loyalty relationships that it offered could not be honored. Abandoning it left

(Continued)

people feeling betrayed and cynical, but it kept IBM from being another Kodak.

Today there is no generally accepted alternative to the traditional talent management model. Even as HR functions have been redesigned to operate as "strategic business partners" or "centers of excellence," talent management remains the same as it always has been, and the same tools are used. Everyone is simply asked to perform better. One of the reasons we feel strongly about telling the Netflix story is the way they have thrown out the old rule book and created a radical new approach to talent management.

Talent management is a particularly critical determinant of an organization's agility. Not only must agile organizations deal with the traditional issues of hiring, retaining, developing, and incenting their members, they must also create a different culture. In it, employees must embrace rather than resist change and have the skills necessary to support the new activities that change calls for. In addition, when necessary, they must be able to turn over the workforce in ethical and socially acceptable ways.

We have argued elsewhere that agile organizations need a "travel light" approach to talent management. The essence of the "travel light" approach is to acquire and discard talent as needed. According to this strategy, the responsibility for the relationship between individuals and organizations shifts to the individual. Employment is "guaranteed" for only as long as an individual has the skills the organization needs and performs them well. In a turbulent world, this approach has some clear advantages over the career approach. It gives agile organizations great flexibility in recruiting and allows the organization to shift competencies relatively quickly.

Organizations that want to use this approach have to take into account at least two problems. First, the approach challenges traditional ethics and some legal aspects of the hiring relationship. To make it work, organizations need to be clear about their employment deal and their employer brand. They need to be up front about the nature of the relationship lest new recruits assume a more traditional set of expectations. There is also a risk that because some stability in senior management is necessary, a caste system of haves and have-nots may form. Methods to minimize this need to be put in place.

Second, a successful travel light policy requires the development of new, cost-effective approaches to recruiting and orienting new employees. It also requires developing effective management support processes to create engagement with a changing workforce.

Netflix summarizes its HR policies and practices in a PowerPoint presentation available on its website. It is one of the most direct, realistic job previews imaginable. If you want to understand what it's like working at Netflix, the presentation spells it out pretty clearly. Sheryl Sandberg, Facebook's COO, called it "the most important document ever to come out of the [Silicon] Valley."

A major portion of the presentation is devoted to the importance of "freedom and responsibility." Its nod to agility, from an HR perspective, begins with the observation that most companies, as they grow and become more complex, tend to increase the amount of controls they put on people's behavior. It is a rational response under traditional assumptions about people and organizations.

Companies, in their urgency to fuel growth, hire more and more people. But when filling positions quickly is more important than filling positions with quality hires, organizations end up "averaging down" the quality of their talent base. To maintain high quality and reliable performance in the face of an average talent pool, organizations implement processes and controls to reduce thinking and problem solving, increase speed and efficiency, and decrease mistakes. And this generally works. The freethinking, high-performing employees leave, while the rule followers who drive a more reliable organization remain. This is great until the market changes. Too late, the organization realizes that it has selected people who are good at following the rules but not so good at flexibility and problem solving. These are the HR dynamics that underlie the thrashing performance pattern.

The best solution, according to Netflix's way of thinking, is to always hire great people and give them more freedom and responsibility, not more rules to follow. The organization's responsibility is to develop and enforce only those rules that speak to integrity and ethics in behavior and prevent "irrevocable disaster." In other words, implement the kinds of processes that help great people achieve great things, and don't implement processes that prevent great people from making recoverable mistakes. If employees cannot make honest mistakes, they cannot learn. If great people cannot learn, they leave. If they leave, you cannot adapt. Hire great people and treat them like adults. What an approach to talent management!

Although every large organization has some kind of performance management system, traditional systems make it difficult to change in significant and important ways. As a result, some critics advocate dismantling and tossing out the whole process and system. We, however, think these systems can be one of the most important levers for agility. Rapid, successful change requires frequent alteration of what people do and, often, of the skills that they have. One way to help ensure that this change occurs is to have a flexible performance management system designed to support organizational change.

Within their freedom and responsibility framework, Netflix applies all of the principles of good performance management systems. It establishes clear goals that are aligned with the strategy, clear expectations of how objectives will be achieved, constant feedback to organizational members on performance, and incentives and recognition for results. What they don't do is get bogged down in turning each of these processes into a formal system or process. Chief Talent Officer Tawni Cranz explained: "We don't have a formal process mainly because it's too restrictive. By the time we sit down and do some kind of formal process, it's likely to change. It's more about hiring the right leader and giving them the right business challenges. And if you set the context and responsibility for each [leader], they're going to nail it."

Alignment, Context, and Transparency

Freedom and responsibility entail a negotiation process. What each individual wants to do (freedom) needs to be aligned with what is best and right for the organization (responsibility). Netflix expects individuals to understand the context of their work and wants them to spend time with their teams worrying about the right objectives, not worrying about which goal setting or performance management form to fill out. Getting alignment on direction is what's important. Cranz says,

> I think we do a couple of things to help them. First, we program time to talk about it every quarter. Every person walks out of our quarterly business reviews with a high-level understanding of what's important in, for example, international, including what's working, what's not working, what are the next steps, how we are thinking about the next market expansion. After the meeting, they piece it together and say, "Okay, well if that's the high level, this is what I contribute, that's my responsibility. Let me go make sure my team delivers on this."

> Second, I think we're very good at identifying the prizes. We align around the three to five things that are most important and most likely to increase our likelihood of winning. And when you're disciplined around that, you don't send people off down a bunch of rabbit holes and waste a bunch of time.

Netflix believes all managers should be good leaders, and all leaders should be good managers. They do not separate the two. We call this a *shared leadership* approach, because it sets the expectation that anyone can take initiative, make decisions, and influence others, in line with the firm's identity and strategic intent. "The best managers figure out how to get great outcomes by setting the appropriate context, rather than by trying to control their people." Context setting involves transparently communicating and discussing strategy, assumptions, roles, knowledge of the stakes in the game, and metrics and objectives. One Netflix executive put it this way:

> I remember my first week-long off-site where we talked about strategy points. We spent more time talking about the cultural values and the meta aspects of running the company than the actual strategy. And I was struck by, "Wow, this is a lot of time with 'expensive' people stuck in a room debating through the finer points." My first reaction was, "What a waste of time," but what I've learned is that it's that constant reinvestment in optimizing how we work, what our values are, that has led us to where we are, which I think is a cultural state as a competitive differentiator. In a sense, I have this confidence that we'll get better at it.

Leadership is a critical "organization capacity" in agile organizations. Netflix develops this capacity by giving people the opportunity to develop themselves, by surrounding them with great colleagues, and giving them big challenges to work on. It is mediocre colleagues and unchallenging work that kills a leader's development.

Although many alignment and context-setting conversations begin within the executive team, that doesn't mean the discussions are private or protected. Far from it. Consistent with a strong perceiving routine, information is highly transparent. Netflix tries to put its most sensitive information in the hands of those doing the work. They recognize that it is a risk and that it is hard work, but they also believe it is important and related to trust as part of the freedom and responsibility framework. Ultimately, Netflix believes they gain more by sharing information than by not sharing it. Chief Talent Officer Cranz shared these ideas with us:

> I think our culture of transparency and sharing information versus retaining and hiding information serves us well. Quarterly business review discussions are cascaded to the rest of the organization. It keeps everyone current with the business threats, wins, and challenges; it iterates and brings people along with you. What's neat is that employees get as deep as they want to get. So if you're a product specialist and you work on the streaming platform engineering team, maybe you're super interested in what's happening in content or maybe you just want the content industry update. You

get to sort of feed your own appetite around what you're interested in and what aligns with the work that you're doing.

Cranz explained that feedback—from team members, supervisors, managers, or customers—is part of that transparency:

> So while there isn't a formal process, there's definitely a feedback mechanism. If you're an engineer or you're a deal maker on the content team or a marketing exec, you get feedback from all of your peers and your regional team, you get it regularly from your boss, and you also get it from your subordinates. It's the nature of our culture to give feedback all the time, because people feel like they need to weigh in to get the best product or the best result or the best service or the best marketing.

Compensation

Bonuses, salaries, stock, and benefits are all important in attracting and retaining individuals, but the mix of rewards may differ greatly from one agile organization to another. Netflix pays its professional employees at or above market rates and expects everyone to perform at high levels. It creates high pay by giving them a high base pay that people can take as either cash or stock. The company does not use bonus plans or variable compensation. Bonus plans and stock options are commonly used by other companies as a way to motivate performance and ensure that the best performers are the most highly paid. In contrast, Netflix pays everyone a top rate, and if they perform poorly, Netflix invokes one of its talent management principles: "Adequate performers get a generous severance package."

When it comes to changes in pay, Netflix does not make adjustments on a calendar basis; they are made on a changing market basis. Netflix looks at each of their individual contributors as having a market—not the market for people doing the same job, but the market for an individual's skills and expertise—and the company is open to increasing the pay of any employee at any time that they believe the market for that individual's skills has changed. It encourages individuals to test the market to find out what they are worth and bring it to management's attention if they feel they deserve an increase. Pay increases occur only when the market changes and/or when individuals acquire new and valuable skills.

Netflix believes that paying above market for employees not only makes practical sense but sends a strong message to everyone about the advantages and disadvantages of working at Netflix. It fits with their corporate culture and aspiration to be a company that is known for seeking excellence, a culture that values high performance, and compensation at the top of the market. It also helps justify their policy of letting go average performers and those whose skills are no longer needed.

The people Netflix hires figure out the freedom-and-responsibility thing pretty quickly, but it does take some "deprogramming" if they come from more traditional companies. For example, if a new marketing leader is hired from an agency and charged with leading a big global campaign from beginning to end, the leader may walk up to a more senior leader and ask, "Who approves this?" However, she realizes pretty quickly that no one has to approve the expenditures. She is the one choosing to spend the money. Similarly, an engineer may bet on using one coding process over another or choosing one production schedule over another. Everyone is expected to make a bet. One manager told us, "You make your bets and you spend your dollars, and now let's see what happens. And that's what we push, that feeling of, 'Wow, I really need to do an amazing job because there are not a lot of people checking and approving everything.' You end up wanting to do all your best work up front because of it."

The Netflix approach is not for everyone, and that is exactly what an agile organization wants: an employer brand that is clear and aligned with the identity of the organization. Such clarity ensures that the right diversity of talent, skills, and values reaches the organization, supports implementation and execution, and remains in the organization as long as they are needed.

The Change Capability at Netflix

The *change capability* is the core of the implementing routine. Like agility, a change capability is a dynamic capability that allows an organization to solve problems and change a firm's resources and processes.[19] But a change capability is not as broad and comprehensive as agility. A change capability is like a very strong muscle that doesn't know whether to push or pull. In concert with the strategizing, perceiving, and testing routines, the change capability is the primary method of new capability development and a powerful contributor to sustained performance. Netflix has demonstrated an amazing capacity to change its core capability sets.

In concert with the strategizing, perceiving, and testing routines, the change capability is the primary method of new capability development and a powerful contributor to sustained performance.

In general, Netflix's approaches to change and capability building involve determining what new skills and knowledge and technology are necessary and how the organization should acquire them. A Netflix executive describes it:

> One of the disciplines that we do have is figuring out what hard problems we are trying to solve, and does the ability to solve it live within our organization. If it doesn't, where should we go buy it? This discipline helps us be honest with ourselves in terms of how much time to invest in a person versus whether or not it's more beneficial for the company to go buy it. When we did a 180-degree pivot in our marketing, we didn't pretend that the people existed in the organization, and so we changed out the whole marketing team over a year. It was a very new problem, and we had to go buy that talent.

Whether an organization goes outside for skills and knowledge or looks inside, what's important is that it is close enough to its talent to know their abilities. With that understanding, it can give them challenging assignments.

Netflix understands that changing and building capabilities require developing muscle around performing new behaviors, and that performing new behaviors well takes practice. Through its freedom-and-responsibility approach, teams have the freedom to build that muscle. When organizations face extreme uncertainty, they can waste a lot of time and money planning and producing plans that are dead on arrival. Extensive planning often is a futile attempt to know the unknowable. The more important activity, after establishing a clear direction (context setting and alignment), is creating the capacity to (1) act, (2) learn quickly whether or not the actions have a positive or negative effect, and (3) be able to set up new actions based on the learnings.

When organizations face extreme uncertainty, they can waste a lot of time and money planning and producing plans that are dead on arrival. Extensive planning often is a futile attempt to know the unknowable.

Action creates the most relevant information and decreases uncertainty. It doesn't release the organization from the need to explore the future, but it makes it easier to think about implementation. The difference between testing and implementing is scale. *Tests* are "low-cost probes"[20] that help to manage risk. *Implementation* is full-scale change that must be embedded in an organization with processes and HR systems to ensure execution. Netflix gives people the freedom to test on a small scale, implement on a large scale, and learn constantly. Netflix doesn't just talk about change; they lean into it and learn from it. One senior manager told us, "Part of what we attempt to inculcate from a cultural and operational perspective is just the idea that things are constantly changing."

The evolution of Netflix's distribution capability represents an important example of constant change (see Exhibit 4.5). Other maps could describe changes in its digital rights and licensing capabilities, its production capabilities, and its marketing capabilities. The point is that Netflix has made a variety of "bet the farm" choices, including moving from physical distribution to streaming, from streaming other people's content to streaming its own content, and from streaming through other networks to developing its own content delivery network. In each case, the organization believed that a revenue stream was going to flatten out or go away or was at risk, and it had to build a new set of capabilities to defend an existing profit stream or support a new one.

Netflix's first new capability implementation was its most hazardous. When the organization shifted from physical to digital distribution, Netflix did not yet have a full-blown change and capability building routine. From a skills and knowledge perspective, the organization needed to add digital storage, streaming, hosting, and other technical skills to its physical distribution know-how. To leverage the new know-how, it had to develop processes for hosting and delivering movies and content developed by others as well as orchestrating the relationship between the two original businesses. This included building relationships and developing licensing arrangements with studios and other content developers. But Netflix did not know how to fully test the proposed changes with customers or how to manage the changes in the media.

Netflix had to learn—and, to its credit, the evidence is that they learned very quickly. They had systems in place to gather customer feedback, and they used them, first to apologize for the way the price

EXHIBIT 4.5. *The Evolution of Netflix Capabilities*

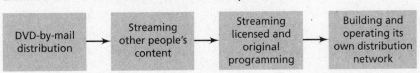

changes were handled and second to acknowledge that Qwikster was the wrong idea. A more recent change in the organization demonstrates how far they have come. On November 13, 2013, Netflix launched a major overhaul of its services website, "the biggest update to its TV experience in the company's history," including better catalog discovery routines and more efficient title displays and summaries. A *USA Today* article noted that Netflix "has been quietly testing it out on several hundred thousand U.S. customers, and the changes have resulted in greater member engagement."[21] Lesson learned.

The second capability building implementation—the move from streaming licensed content to delivering a full range of licensed and original programming—was more about developing production and marketing capabilities. In starting up its original programming, Netflix decided it was best to have an internal leader. It appointed someone with an outstanding deal-making history, who had successfully led and managed programming for the streaming business, and who had demonstrated creativity in the past.

Netflix could have gone outside and bought ready-made expertise; there was plenty of interest in the labor marketplace when the word got out that Netflix was looking for a new head of original programming. The organization's interest in doing something different led them to make the choice not to go outside. In time, it had to acquire the ability to generate, evaluate, and choose scripts, produce episodes, market original programming, and so on. A wholly new set of work processes, labor relations, and marketing processes had to be developed and integrated.

Recently, Netflix decided to change its distribution model again. It went from storing and streaming content from other servers to streaming from its own network. The impetus for this move was the recognition of a threat to its profit stream and business model, the result of an effective strategizing and perceiving routine.

Netflix's current success rests on a critical assumption that is associated with the principle of net neutrality. The principle maintains that governments and internet service providers, such as AT&T, Comcast, or Orange, should treat all data on the Internet equally. There should be no discrimination or different charging schemes based on user, content, site, platform, or application. However, to improve the Netflix customer experience, all the movies and games and programs it distributes need to be as close to the user as possible. In order to accomplish this, much of Netflix's content was stored on commercially owned and operated content delivery networks (CDNs). These servers are placed around the world. They charge Netflix a fee for storage.

If the commercial CDNs or ISPs actively look to increase revenues or exercise control over traffic flows—a big concern under net neutrality —Netflix's business model and customer experience could be affected negatively. As a result, Netflix decided, in much the same way that YouTube did, to build its own CDN, host its own content on its own servers, and make it accessible to customers through the ISPs.

Greg Peters heads the CDN initiative even though he has never built a CDN. However, because of his demonstrated leadership inside Netflix, his technical knowledge, and, perhaps most important, because of his predilection for change and challenge, he was given the go-ahead to build a team and figure it out. In two years, he has built a team of internal people, rounded out their experiences with key external hires, and put Netflix on every platform around the world.

Peters talked about how changing and learning were a central part of building the capability:

> There is always an opportunity to ask the question, "Are we optimally suited to meet the challenges in front of us, and if not, what can we change to address that?" Nobody gets to bank on things being static; that shouldn't be an expectation that people have. Building a culture around [challenging the way things are] allows us to have more functional discussions around change that reduce politics and parochial interests that often encumber other companies. It creates an environment where anybody can say at a given point in time there's an opportunity to do things better. It's less about the personal success or how to accumulate people or power, but more about how to work with your peers to find those optimal solutions and move forward.

The change capability at Netflix integrates the HR philosophy of freedom and responsibility with the business realities of technology, customers, and marketing. To build new capabilities, individuals must be willing and able to take on new things, learn new things, and develop new skills. Netflix ensures that the organization is ready to change by hiring people with an appetite for it and a comfort with ambiguity and uncertainty. They have built a strong bench—from executives to directors to the HR team—that has very good skill sets for managing change. "It has become the norm in our culture to embrace change. Change is celebrated. It isn't feared." But at Netflix there is more than just a skill set or comfort with ambiguity; there is a change architecture, a way of thinking about how to build new capabilities through learning that makes it an agile organization.

CONCLUSION

In combination with strategizing and perceiving, the testing and implementing routines make two important contributions to agile organizations. First, the testing routine provides the ability to select from among a set of potential responses: (1) the ones most likely to contribute to the current strategic intent, (2) the means to establish a new set of capabilities, or (3) the framework of a new strategy. Second, with the implementing routine, organizations have the capacity to embed new responses, capabilities, and strategies in the organization. The implementing routine also complements the other agility routines by keeping the existing organization running smoothly and maintaining the workforce capacity needed to adapt.

CHAPTER

5

TRANSFORMING TO AGILITY

It is a bad plan that admits of no modification.

—PUBLILIUS SYRUS, FIRST CENTURY B.C.

In our research, organizations that possess the routines of agility—strategizing, perceiving, testing, and implementing—consistently outperformed their industry peers over long periods of time. Organizations that did not have these routines exhibited profit performance patterns that either thrashed about the industry mean as they were buffeted by environmental forces or chronically underperformed the industry mean as if their energies were spent. In our financial database of 424 firms, only 18 percent of them could meet the 80-percent standard of above-average profitability, and in our survey database, where we tried to find agile organizations, less than 30 percent had three or more above-average routines.

Is there hope for the thrashers and underperformers? What can they do to alter their fate?

AN ORIENTATION TO TRANSFORMATION

The answer to the first question is a qualified "yes." Agility does not come quickly or easily, and in many ways it is never over. The transformation to agility is not like a turnaround. First, it takes longer; second, it is developmental. The transformation to agility may deliver a return to reasonable performance levels if done right. However, if it is done wrong, if the routines of agility are not patiently built on a solid foundation of dynamic management practice and a set of differentiating capabilities, the organization will be unable to sustain the improvement in performance. It is likely to remain among the ranks of the thrashers.

Developmentally, agile organizations are built on good management practices and processes designed to support a higher level of functioning than those found in traditional organizations. These practices and processes deliver objectivity, transparency, timeliness, flexibility, and accountability so that decisions are consistently based on relevant facts. This is not as easy as it sounds, and such practices are rarer than you might think.

Even after years of work, the managers at every agile organization we have worked with say the same thing: "We still have so much to learn." That's because the proof of agility is in the results, not in some management writer's use of a specific practice as evidence of agility. An organization with a good innovation process or with effective and agile leaders or a flexible resource allocation system is not an agile organization. Being agile means having all those things and above-average profitability more than 80 percent of the time for a long period; it means you have implemented a variety of significant changes and not lost a beat. It can be done, as the DaVita story in Chapter One and the Harley-Davidson story that closes this chapter demonstrate, but it takes years.

Even after years of work, the managers at every agile organization we have worked with say the same thing: "We still have so much to learn."

The answer to the second question—what can an organization do?—can also be answered with qualifications. Every transformation to agility that we are aware of followed a path that was unique. It always involved some diagnosis to determine gaps, weaknesses, and places to start. Based on that diagnosis, the timing, sequence, and specific initiatives depended on the resources and situation at hand. Based on our observations, most transformations to agility touch three broad categories of change:

1. Setting the strategy

2. Fixing the foundation

3. Building the agility routines

Setting the Strategy

An organization's strategy includes both short- and long-term elements—intent and identity. What the organization has to get right, right away, is the development and deployment of a clear strategic intent. It is the single biggest driver of current performance.

This entails articulating a clear economic logic, developing a set of competitive differentiators, and then designing and implementing management systems that allow everyone to play their part in execution. However, because environments change, strategy is a wasting asset. Organizations should not overinvest in making the intent perfect; it just needs to be good enough to drive decisions about management processes, structures, and systems.

Much more difficult than getting the intent right—and requiring much more time to achieve—is the task of changing the organization's identity, if it needs changing. The important diagnostic issue is whether or not the organization's identity is change-friendly. If the organization is not agile, the transformation to agility usually requires some modification of its identity to make it more change-friendly. Such an identity is central to the ongoing adaptation of the organization. It supports robust strategic intents and signals the organization to expect changes to structure, capabilities, and other systems.

Identities, like culture, emerge over time and cannot be changed directly. It requires a serious commitment on the part of the top management team (TMT) to change the organization and themselves. First, the organization must continually reinforce the new identity by applying the ITSS principle ("It's the system, stupid"). Managers must design every change in structure, management practice, or system in such a way that it supports the new identity and the other elements of organization design. A new incentive system must not contradict the values or brand implied by the identity, and it must align with measurement systems and structures. Second, management must demonstrate the new identity through consistent communication, behaviors, and decisions. The process of changing may outlast the tenure of senior executives and even the CEO. As a result, a new identity is more of a lagging variable than a leading indicator of the transformation to agility.

Research suggests that embedding a robust, changeable strategic intent and a change-friendly identity can be accelerated.[1] Involving people in the changes that affect them accelerates ownership of the new intent and identity. Establishing learning processes and mechanisms speeds behavioral change, and finally, decentralizing local implementation speeds overall change. These tried-and-true principles are often forgotten or ignored.

Fixing the Foundation

Organizations that wish to improve their profit performance by becoming more agile must first master the basic "blocking and tackling" of management. Organizations that adopt the latest management fad with the word "agile" attached to it do not understand the fundamentals of agility. They are ignoring the ITSS principle and the importance of good management practices that are the foundation of the agile capability. Systems thinking (another way of stating the ITSS principle) and an appreciation of the complex interplay among good management practices—such as setting goals, establishing effective structures, managing information flows, and designing incentives—are what separate organizations with effective management systems from those with ineffective ones. Even the best people cannot overcome the constraints imposed by bad systems.

It all begins with strategy. The economic logic of the strategy determines what operational measures of performance drive profitability. Planning and performance management systems should be built around these measures and follow a plan-do-check-act or Shewhart cycle, a process named after the father of statistical process control, that establishes targets, regularly monitors performance, and makes adjustments when actual results diverge from plans. Too often, these systems fail because managements measure the wrong things, fail to complete the Shewhart cycle, or fail to design the systems with flexibility in mind.

Building the Agility Routines

To be agile means knowing how capabilities are built. It always involves acquiring or developing the appropriate skills and knowledge. Every capability is grounded in know-how that can be quite specific; subtle differences that may be critical are often overlooked. Capabilities also require an appropriate architecture to support the repeated application of the skills. Structures, workflows, and systems must be designed that allow behaviors to drive the necessary outcomes. Finally, no capability emerges from the planning process fully baked; it requires trials, failures, and eventual successes. The organization must embrace and engineer the messy experiences that come with learning how to perform the capability well.

Most important, agility requires that large, complex organizations be able to quickly and reliably change as conditions merit. This may seem obvious. Agile organizations can adapt to and initiate change, and they do both with intention. This is the value of the *implementing routine* and its embedded change management capability. These companies have legacies of successful IT system rollouts, merger integrations, reorganizations, and business transformations because they invested in disciplined processes, objective measurement, sound governance, and management accountability that deliver results as anticipated. Without the implementing routine, even organizations with strong strategizing, perceiving, and testing routines will struggle to deliver agility, or perhaps even to deliver improved performance.[2]

Two large organizations, Cambia Health Solutions and Allstate Insurance, recently initiated transformation journeys that reflect the use of all three categories of change. The Cambia case is instructive because their transformation design focused on "fixing the foundation." They chose to build more sophisticated and flexible management processes and worked from the bottom of the Agility Pyramid up. In addition, they paid attention to ITSS as part of their management of identity change. Their efforts paid significant dividends after only two years of work.

Allstate Insurance employed a different set of accelerated change techniques to improve performance, build more effective routines, and embed a change capability in the organization. They too applied the ITSS principle to local units in the hope that an overall transformation might follow.

CAMBIA HEALTH SOLUTIONS

Few environments have undergone as much upheaval and public scrutiny over the past thirty years as has the health care industry. Over that time, health care costs ballooned, growing faster than GDP for a decade. Today, the United States spends twice as much on health care per capita as any other OECD country, yet health care outcomes are among the worst. A Republican Congress beat back the Clinton universal health care initiative of the early 1990s, but the Patient Protection and Affordable Care Act of 2010 (aka "Obamacare") brought a whole new set of regulatory changes. Universal access to health insurance forced the carriers, health care providers, and pharmaceutical companies to respond to a new set of environmental pressures. Having avoided a single-payer model like those employed in the UK, Canada, and Japan, the industry was expected to become part of the solution to runaway costs and suboptimal outcomes.

Regence is the Blue Cross Blue Shield health insurance affiliate of Cambia Health Solutions in the states of Washington, Oregon, Idaho, and Utah. It is a ninety-year-old company with a strong reputation for integrity and customer service, but as a member of a highly regulated industry, it had developed a conservative culture embedded in a hierarchical, command-and-control organization structure.

In 2004, Regence's board and senior leaders, led by CEO Mark Ganz, responded to and anticipated many of the environmental changes by establishing a new corporate vision. It was dubbed "The Cause: To serve as a catalyst in transforming health care, creating a person-focused and economically sustainable system." By 2010, Ganz had architected a significant reorganization, creating a parent holding company to house Regence Health Insurance, the traditional Blue Cross Blue Shield business, and Direct Health Solutions (DHS), an incubator business charged with developing or investing in innovative products and services, such as pharmacy benefits; disability; dental, vision, and other lines of insurance; alternative forms of health care access; and freestanding health and wellness solutions. Both Regence and the DHS organizations focused on serving The Cause. In 2011, Regence changed the name of the parent company to Cambia Health Solutions, allowing the new DHS start-ups to be viewed as separate from the traditional Blue Cross Blue Shield Regence brand.

The restructuring and change in strategy led to tensions in the organization. The Cause, by itself, was an insufficient statement of strategic intent to guide planning and decision making. The investments in the DHS companies, which were expected to achieve a higher rate of return than the insurance business, suggested to some that economic sustainability had become the driving force behind Cambia, to the detriment of member satisfaction. The management attention given to DHS left some people in Regence feeling like the emphasis had suddenly shifted away from the company they had built.

Cambia is a sponsor company of the Center for Effective Organizations at USC and was aware of our research into organization agility. In late 2010, they asked for some help with culture change to ensure that their investments would make them more fit for the future.

An agility assessment, consisting of a broadly administered survey coupled with structured management interviews, was conducted at Cambia in the spring of 2011. On the positive side, there was a strong sense of shared purpose, captured by The Cause, across the organization, and a belief that the structure reflected that purpose. There was also consensus that Cambia was a values-driven company that emphasized a strong "member focus."

On the negative side, people feared that The Cause was too grand a mission for employees to embrace and too bold for an organization with Cambia's limited capabilities. Innovation, in particular, was essential to the new strategy and The Cause. However, diagnostic interviews revealed a deep frustration that it was "hard to get things done" at Cambia. A lack of empowerment and accountability meant that decisions were pushed up for resolution. These symptoms were indicative of more fundamental problems. Management systems—such as goal setting, information flows, and decision making—reflected the hierarchical silos of the Regence Health business and did not support an implied strategy of risk-taking in the service of new product and service development. People in general did not understand how their individual goals connected to the strategy, were not held accountable for outcomes, and did not experience either positive or negative consequences for their performance. Finally, Cambia lacked a change management capability. For example, the IT organization had a poor reputation, and a recent complex systems changeover served as an example of poor execution that was producing a number of headaches around the organization.

Cambia's CEO, Mark Ganz, understood that the diagnosis seriously threatened its ability to execute the strategy, and he commissioned the VP of HR, Mark Stimpson, to address these important issues.

Stimpson pulled together a design team to review the findings of the agility assessment. In addition to a broad plan for thinking about identity change consistent with the original mandate of looking at culture, they commissioned four task forces to:

- Develop a clear, shared process for setting organizational objectives and communicating those objectives

- Design and implement a common change management process

- Revise the human capital and performance management processes

- Explore in greater detail the notion that it "was hard to get stuff done" at Cambia and propose solutions

Initiating the Identity Journey

The strategy and structure changes that preceded the diagnosis were changing the organization's culture. On that point everyone agreed, but the agility assessment pushed Cambia's leadership to think more broadly and to become more intentional about shaping the emerging culture and identity.

Stimpson enlisted the help of Cambia's marketing and communications groups to discover the existing identity and plan for managing the emergence of a new one. Employee focus groups were used to identify the cultural values associated with The Cause. To everyone's relief, they aligned with Cambia's aspirational values, including accountability, agility, commitment, innovation, trust, teamwork, nonprofit status, and leadership. From the brand/image side, the Regence brand was not as well known as the Blue Cross Blue Shield brand and trailed some competitors in other attributes, such as community involvement and patient advocacy, which were central to The Cause. However, the Regence brand did have several positive attributes on which to build, including trust, good customer service, a comprehensive provider network, and overall value.

While Cambia was generally values driven, there was no consensus about an identity label. The tagline, "Members first," came closest, but no one felt it was quite right, and most people agreed that its regulated history probably meant the identity was not change-friendly. In addition, the organization's aspirational values did not line up with the diagnostic data, which suggested that the organization struggled with accountability, innovation, teamwork, and change. These data became important inputs to the task force initiatives. As the design team was chartering the task forces, it established mechanisms for them to coordinate with each other and required that proposed solutions should support the organization's aspirational values to present a unified front about the direction of change. In addition, involving the marketing and communications groups made them aware of building the company's brand with these issues in mind. In this way, Cambia hoped to drive the emergence of a more change-friendly identity.

Designing and Implementing the Initiatives

The change process at Cambia was deliberate and insightful. The design team recognized that if agility was to become a way of life in the organization, the change process could not be a new "program" or "project." Their approach was to make organization change within the context of existing systems and processes. Instead of a new objective setting and communications system, they would understand the pros and cons of the existing system, make deliberate and powerful changes to it, and then continuously make tweaks and reforms. Instead of announcing a new performance management system, they would work within the existing system and change it from the inside out. Change would be significant but evolutionary, not discontinuous.

The change process at Cambia was deliberate and insightful. They recognized that if agility was to become a way of life, the change process could not be a new "program"... they made deliberate and powerful changes to existing systems.

A design team member led each task force, which consisted of four to seven VPs and directors drawn from across Cambia's business leaders. The teams were chartered with specific objectives, resources, and time frames for completion. For example, the human capital and performance management task force consisted of the OD director, an HR director, and five line leaders, all of whom had strong opinions on how to improve the current approach. It was chartered to recommend performance management process changes that aligned with the organization's values for all management and supervisory positions (approximately 750 people).

After careful review, the task force recommended a system of quarterly objectives and performance reviews to replace the annual system that reviewed conformance with a generic set of required behaviors. The linchpin of the new process was the quarterly "performance conversation" between leaders and their direct reports to review progress against goals and prepare for the following quarter. The process was modeled on one used by other leaders who found it effective for both business results and personal development. The "conversations" included both *what* the objectives were and whether or not they were achieved, and *how* achievement of the objectives reflected the desired organizational values. A key component of these conversations was validating that the objectives currently being worked on were still the right ones, while still retaining the option to stop working on them, start new ones, or continue on course.

The task force also recommended changes to the annual performance evaluation process. The first was to reduce the number of performance categories from four to two (performing and exceeding), although they recognized that a "needs improvement" category would have to be included. The second was to ensure that the spread of merit pay increases between "performers" and "exceeders" remained differentiated. Annually, exceeders could get two-and-a-half times the increases associated with performers.

In addition, the task force recommended a "spot" rewards program for all leadership positions to acknowledge exemplary performance in a timely and public fashion. The Excellence in Leadership Award recognized leaders for excellence in human capital management or demonstration of agile behaviors. The award itself was $1,000 in cash, presented personally by a member of Cambia's leadership team, and a write-up in the company newsletter.

Implementation of the new process involved a broad range of communication and management support. The task force presented the proposed changes at Cambia's annual senior leadership summit. The leaders were then provided a timetable for their own initial quarterly objectives and for those of the rest of management across the company. Online training in human capital management, performance conversations, and SMART (specific, measurable, achievable, relevant, and timely) objectives was made available. In addition, implementation coaches, including the CEO as a coach for his direct reports, were assigned to oversee the implementation of the process, remove roadblocks, and hold leaders accountable to put the new process in place. By the deadline, 90 percent of leadership had submitted their quarterly objectives and participated in the mandatory online training.

The three other task forces also made progress to varying degrees over the course of the year.

- The Organizational Objectives task force developed a standard process and calendar that integrated the board-level strategic planning cycle with the new performance management system.

- The Change Management task force developed a shared model and process that was piloted in several groups and approved by the Cambia Leadership Team. Task force members and others trained in the process served as sponsors who worked with business managers to teach them the model and apply it to ongoing changes in their units. An embedded and shared way of thinking about change was taking place.

- The "Hard to Get Stuff Done" task force confirmed the findings of the original diagnostic but could not put their finger on a solution. Part of the issue concerned *who* was in a particular role or position. Their data suggested that if the "right" people were in the job, they "made it happen," found "work-arounds," and "busted through the bureaucracy." It was an important learning for the design team—

one that was diffused through the organization—that it was the organization's design that made work and achieving results hard. The design team needed to focus attention on designing and implementing a system in which it was easy to get things done. An important outcome was a commitment to look at how decision rights were allocated in the organization and whether an effective decision-making process was in place.

In addition to these changes, Cambia's CEO brought in new senior leaders by replacing existing leaders, creating new roles, or backfilling retirements. These new leaders outwardly embraced the proposed changes in strategy and operating philosophy and displayed leadership styles that were aligned to agility, The Cause, and the values. Often the best way to manage change is to *change the management*. The benefits were twofold. First, it brought in leaders who possessed those transformational skills the CEO and the organization needed. Second, those leaders began to hire people like themselves, thus multiplying the number of leaders with these needed skills. All of these moves sent strong signals to the organization that the most senior executives were serious about implementing the changes they talked about; they were "walking the talk."

Ganz also restructured a corporate leadership team that was too large to be effective. Prior to 2011, Cambia's management system included a governing body called the SPG, which was generally understood to mean Strategic Planning Group. Its purpose, responsibilities, membership, and decision authority were generally related to communication and planning rather than decision making. It included the market presidents of the four Blue Cross Blue Shield state plans, the CFO, and other direct reports to the CEO, as well as numerous indirect reports to the CEO.

Following the diagnostic survey and interviews, the CEO disbanded the SPG and replaced it with four management forums, each with clear membership, decision rights, and alignment to The Cause. The first was the corporate leadership team, which consisted of the direct reports of the CEO and the HR VP. The second team consisted of the leadership team for Regence Health, the third was the leadership team for DHS, and the fourth was the shared services team that provided internal support to Regence Health and DHS.

Reflections

Cambia's approach to their transformation serves as a valuable model and reflects all of the change categories described earlier. In setting the strategy, The Cause was an important if incomplete statement of strategic intent. Fortunately, Cambia had the luxury of time; this was a transformation of choice, not of necessity. They had started the change well ahead of the pressures brought on by the Affordable Care Act. Knowing the limits of the organization's conservative culture and capabilities, Cambia approached change incrementally, built on small successes to gain momentum, involved a large number of people in planning and implementing the change, and decentralized much of the implementation.

At the identity level, they accelerated change by focusing on the ITSS principle. No one change was made in isolation, every change was made with a cross-functional team and a member of the design team so that the changes were made in parallel and as a system, and every change was made in alignment with The Cause and the values the organization was trying to instill. Such a process should help accelerate the emergence of a change-friendly identity.

Cambia also applied the principles of good management to fix the foundation as part of its transformation. They focused on things that got people's attention. The planning and performance management systems began the important process of changing behavior. This may not seem like much, but in an organization so burdened with inertia, it is no small thing to implement changes that directly affect the way every manager and supervisor is evaluated and compensated. Yet they got the commitment of the entire top management team through enlistment or replacement, and they involved them in the implementation.

Cambia employed the plan-do-check-act cycle with each of the task forces and supported the building of a learning capability. The design team monitored progress to plan and handled reporting to senior management. They regularly reviewed the progress of initiatives and determined if they should continue, because they were adding value, or stop, because they were not adding value or because implementation was sufficient. They also determined if new initiatives should be started because something important was missing. One year into implementation, the design team commissioned a review that included a short survey and interviews with a variety of stakeholders. The findings and recommendations from the review were fed back into the project plan for the next phases of activities. The high level of communication and engagement helped reinforce staff commitment to the changes in operating processes as well as encouraged innovation and risk-taking.

Two-and-a-half years later, a major resurvey of the top leaders found significant improvements in all the dimensions of agility. Most important, the biggest improvements came in the areas of greatest weakness, including robust strategies, change, innovation, learning capabilities, information transparency, and flexible resource allocation. Reflecting the continuing nature of the identity journey, leaders' ratings of the extent to which the identity was change-friendly increased significantly, although this remained among the lower scores. In addition, respondents reported increased frequencies of behaviors that were considered key to The Cause and the organization's values.

Is Cambia agile at this point? There is always a temptation to declare victory when survey results suggest impressive improvement. But as almost every Cambia leader we interviewed emphasized, "We have come a long way, and there's still a long way to go." While several key dimensions that constitute the agile routines are nearing benchmark levels for the financial services sector, they cannot yet claim above-average scores for at least three of the routines. So, no, they haven't arrived yet. However, as we mentioned at the beginning of this chapter, agility is a long-term journey. The proof will be in Cambia's performance and with the emergence and recognition of a change-friendly identity. But they have made significant changes in the way they operate and have laid the foundation for becoming an innovator in the health care industry. This foundation will be an important part of their improving on the four agility routines. Their chances for success will be a function of senior management's collective ability to maintain their commitment to see the change through and make it deliver results.

ALLSTATE INSURANCE COMPANY

The Cambia case was a good example of fixing the foundation, and it demonstrates how redesigning several of the good management practices can support a transformation to agility. Now we focus on the importance of setting the strategy and building the routines. The transformation process at the Allstate Insurance Company employed a series of campaigns aimed at building an enterprise-wide change capability and leadership capacity.

Allstate is an iconic U.S. organization and one of the largest publicly owned property-casualty insurance companies in America. "The good hands people" (the slogan was created in 1950 and is associated with one of the best-known brands in the insurance industry[3]) started as a Sears mail-order business, moved into the retail stores, and grew in spectacular fashion. When Sears diversified in the 1980s, Allstate Insurance became part of the Sears Financial Network that included the Discover credit card, Dean Witter Reynolds investments, and Coldwell Banker real estate. The network was eventually disbanded, and Sears spun off 20 percent of Allstate in 1993 and fully divested the organization in 1995. Since going public, Allstate's profitability has exceeded the industry average only twice in seventeen years. Despite a number of performance-enhancing initiatives, none have taken hold enough to produce sustained results, and this performance pattern led the organization to consider alternative change approaches. Today Allstate is changing from the middle out. Over the past five years and using primarily internal resources, Allstate has conducted a series of transformations in increasingly large and complex units of the company, including I/T, operations, and claims.

Transformation at Allstate has two objectives: (1) to change the performance of the business by changing the way people work, one group at a time, and (2) to build and embed a change management capability in the organization so that implementing new adaptations becomes easier over time. To support the first objective, the transformation process generally followed a common set of phases that map to the categories of setting the strategy, fixing the foundation, and building the routines. The Allstate process involves:

- Challenging unit leadership to undertake the change and clarify unit strategy
- Using inputs from stakeholders and design teams to develop large-group interventions (LGIs) that accelerate the change process
- Sustaining change and organization learning

To support the second objective, Allstate built on its existing Organizational Effectiveness (OE) group. Through internal development experiences and outside hires, the OE group was elevated to a corporate function with high visibility. The OE group has a mandate to lead the transformation process, build differentiating routines, and see that the changes are sustained.

Building any differentiating capability is difficult, resource intensive, and time-consuming. It entails acquiring the requisite skills and know-how, designing processes that will deliver desired outputs, and deploying tools and infrastructure that will support those processes. But the only way to truly develop an organizational capability is to practice it, apply the know-how, exercise the routines and tools, work out the bugs, and continuously improve performance. New capabilities often start out as pilot projects in one part of the organization, then scale up as they are deployed elsewhere. When operated at scale, they deliver their full value. Valuable capabilities that are hard to duplicate contribute to competitive advantage.

So it is with Allstate's change management capability. It is useful to have it in the corporate OE group, but it is truly differentiating when it can be deployed in all of Allstate's operations. By working with managers to apply a similar set of processes and tools in the transformation of each business, Allstate is building more effective routines and teaching itself how to be good at implementing change.

Challenge Leadership and Clarify Strategy

This strategy-setting process is aimed directly at building more effective strategizing and perceiving routines. The OE team begins each transformation by challenging the leadership of a given group with a simple question: Will the leadership styles and strategies that may have served you in the past serve you in the future? Allstate's traditional culture had military overtones, owing to past executives with armed services backgrounds, and management leaned heavily on a command-and-control style that left little room for initiative and risk-taking. John Bader, a longtime Allstate executive rooted in the traditional culture, was among the first to grasp the extent of the leadership transformation that was required. "I had to let go of everything I had ever been taught and practiced as a leader and had to engage with my people in a completely different leadership mind-set," he said.

Without being overly prescriptive, leaders are expected to define and commit to specific behaviors that support the organization's values of diversity and inclusion as well as engagement, initiative, accountability, and risk-taking. The leadership behaviors required to support effective strategizing and perceiving routines are built on these types of values and beliefs, and the OE team will not support a transformation until the leadership team commits demonstrably to a different style of leading. Paying lip service to these behaviors is not enough.

A leadership team also invests time to define a clear business and functional strategic intent. Reflecting the best of the perceiving routine, leadership teams engage in environmental scanning activities, including gathering data on the "voice of the customer" and inputs from a variety of stakeholders. Based on that data, they develop initial perspectives on the economic logic and breadth, differentiation, and level of aggressiveness that will best deliver on its objectives. For example, the claims' leadership team developed the COMPASS, a "North Star" document that captured the unit's purpose, strategy, and values. The COMPASS recognized important changes in the industry and how those changes affected the claims business model. It was communicated broadly, employed throughout the transformation process, and remains in use today.

Accelerate Change Through Large-Group Interventions

Once the leadership team makes personal commitments to the strategy and their own change, they work with the OE group and other stakeholders to develop a change strategy. This can involve the formation of a design team—a group of diverse unit stakeholders, including sponsors from the leadership team—to conduct a broader diagnosis, design interventions, and monitor and sustain the implementation.

Using a formal design team has risks and advantages. On the risk side, design team members are often skeptical that this time around things will be different. Team-building interventions may be necessary to help them challenge and adjust these attitudes. By understanding their own process of change and trust building, design team members are better able to design and implement a change process for the business. One clear advantage, however, is that when a design team works with a leadership team, the skills and knowledge associated with planning and managing change spread more quickly.

Because LGIs involve a broad range of stakeholders, this strategy allows the business to take a systemic approach to transformation—applying the ITSS principle rather than a piecemeal, one-system-at-a-time approach.

The single most important technique used to accelerate change at Allstate is the large-group intervention (LGI). Variously known as search conferences, open space meetings, or decision accelerators, LGIs vary in purpose (such as visioning, strategy formulation, organization design, or implementation planning); size (from fewer than fifty to over two thousand people); composition (mix of internal and external stakeholders); length (hours or days); structure (very rigid and formal or loose and informal); and number (single events or a series of linked conferences).[4] Although the OE group customizes each transformation strategy, they often use a series of LGIs of about two hundred people to build a vision, define change initiatives, and sustain the transformation. Because LGIs involve a broad range of stakeholders, this strategy allows the business to take a systemic approach to transformation—applying the ITSS principle rather than a piecemeal, one-system-at-a-time approach.

The unit's leadership team, in collaboration with the OE group or the design team, run an initial LGI jointly. Its purpose is to get buy-in for the strategy, refine any diagnostic work done by the leadership team, and establish the vision and case for change. Of particular importance, the first LGI gives the leadership team members an opportunity to demonstrate new behaviors consistent with the new way of operating while soliciting insight and commitment from the group. LGIs teach organization members and stakeholders how to think about shared leadership, perform innovative work, and make multistakeholder decisions—all important components of the agility routines. The output of the first LGI helps to create a vivid picture of the organization's desired future state along several dimensions. Participants are charged with being ambassadors for change in their home subunits.

A second LGI, with new participants from the same business or function, can take the results of the first LGI and propose a set of initiatives that will deliver the desired change. By giving the large group a choice in what to address, the organization can focus on the most important agility routine or redesign the most important good management practices. For example, the customer and enterprise services (CES) unit put forward "Five Bold Moves" that were implemented to support a strategy of "thrilling the customer" and "getting different." They included changes in feedback processes and nonmonetary recognition programs that expected the same behaviors and performance from the printing press operator or an executive, a "travelling employee team" charged with sharing best practices and changing work processes, and training in business acumen. The claims organization launched a number of transformational initiatives, changed the organization structure, and significantly modified a number of backbone processes. Thus the desired output of the second LGI is three to five initiatives with clear objectives and staffing requirements and a clear line of sight to agility. The design team and the leadership team are then jointly tasked with providing resources to the initiatives and monitoring their progress.

Sustain Change and Learn

A third LGI challenges participants to sustain the changes that the various initiatives will deliver. This has three aspects: structural changes, leadership attention, and continuous improvement. Structural changes take the form of organization redesigns, process and workflow changes, information systems changes, or combinations of all three. The OE team brings tools to bear here, such as Galbraith's Star Model for organization design. LGI participants also develop new management processes to ensure that the change initiatives remain front and center on the leadership agenda. For some groups, this means making it a standing item at monthly leadership team meetings.

Finally, the OE team uses this third LGI to develop processes and tools to capture learning from the initiatives, to drive continuous improvements in performance, and to create new knowledge and skills regarding change. For example, the organization has learned that:

○ Methodologies and change initiatives are effective only if they are adopted by the organization. The issue is not whether the OE team can run an LGI or manage a change in work processes, but how to transfer the skills and knowledge to the line organization so that it can run its own change processes. Methods, models, tools, and changes must fit with the organization's reality and be owned by its members. In transformations where the OE team did most of the work because they wanted to be helpful or speed up the pace of change, success was limited.

○ Leaders must understand the required behavior changes and their implications, commit to them, live them, and be held accountable for them. Over the course of different transformations, everyone had to deal with the problem of the "unpopped kernel": a manager who had been given support, resources, feedback, and time but had not demonstrated the new behaviors. When these managers were replaced, it was a very public demonstration of leadership's commitment to the values and the transformation at Allstate. When the "unpopped kernels" were not addressed, trust in leadership and credibility for the change decreased, and the ability to implement change dissolved.

Over the course of different transformations, everyone had to deal with the problem of the "unpopped kernel": a manager who had been given support, resources, feedback, and time but had not demonstrated the new behaviors.

○ Measurement, using concrete data, is an intervention; it is not just a data-gathering process. People pay attention to what's measured, and efforts to change measurement and incentive systems are powerful. These good management practices—shaped to operate in a flexible way—help fix the foundation and support the perceiving and testing routines.

○ Until a tangible shift is experienced in terms of day-to-day work, the change is not perceived to be real. The LGIs allow a higher percentage of people in the organization to participate in the diagnosis, decide on the changes to be made, and commit to the transformation. This alone makes the change more real and owned. But more important, the high degree of freedom given to the LGI participants to choose the meaningful and agility-related changes also ensures that change addresses the real issue of adding value.

As a result, with each transformation, the OE team, each unit's leadership team, design team, and staff are learning about changing a complex system and operating more agile organizations. Each unit going through a transformation implements a variety of changes. Some are successful, some are not, but each change represents an opportunity to learn. It is the essence of the testing routine.

Reflections

The transformation process at Allstate, and especially its heavy use of LGIs, had several key benefits. First, the opening set of activities—challenging leadership and clarifying strategy—speaks loudly about the way the agile organization operates. The strategy and perceiving routines depend greatly on an enlightened view of leading and managing that encourages engagement and speaking truth to power. Committing to new leadership behaviors and employing LGIs represents an inclusive, transparent, and shared view of leadership and focuses on getting clear strategies formulated, shared, and executed quickly. Second, the process focuses on learning, a key component of the testing routine. LGIs teach organization members new skills and knowledge with respect to innovation and multistakeholder decision making.

The process helped the organization implement change quickly and build change capability. LGIs accelerate change by considering a variety of issues simultaneously rather than serially with each stakeholder, tapping into the energy and information of all participants for problem solving and action, and promoting the transformation of ideas into practical action steps through the rapid prototyping of options and alternatives. The pace at which the implementation of a new strategy can occur is set by the ability of the different stakeholders to understand the strategy, their willingness to accept the new capabilities, and their ability to contribute to the change. Large-group interventions bring "the whole system into the room"[5] and can remove and relax these limits through "education by common experience."[6] When a whole system shares and commonly interprets an experience, it can produce significant and rapid changes in understanding and behavior.

Accelerated change processes in turn accelerate the achievement of results. For the operations group, the "green line" of customer satisfaction started to improve. Years had gone by with absolutely no movement in customer satisfaction; after the LGIs, continuous improvement was shown for seven months in a row, moving from 77 percent to 84 percent satisfaction. In addition, the operations group started "paying back" part of its budget each year through cost reductions and improved productivity. Finally, the organization successfully implemented a difficult and large-scale operational change. An evaluation of that change widely attributed its success to the lessons learned from the transformation.

In the Claims organization, less than two years after the transformation began, the customer engagement scores for Allstate, as measured by an outside agency, were up twenty-nine points and had reached the "high satisfaction" tier. Internally, organization engagement scores were up at least five points in eight out of nine categories. Qualitatively, the organization continues to experience shifts in leadership style and improved headquarters–field office relationships, and there is a belief that the field offices are being more proactive in making operational changes.

Is Allstate agile? Not yet. Like Cambia, they have a way to go, but they have put themselves on the right track. Supported by their change-friendly "good hands" identity, they are building a strong and embedded change capability that will allow them to make changes more quickly and efficiently. Their emphasis on changing the leadership mind-sets and conducting the change process to reinforce the emergence of a shared leadership philosophy will support the emergence of a strong perceiving routine. However, their "middle out" change strategy is risky, and its future success depends on the continued support of corporate executives. The success of the transformation in producing meaningful results will certainly help in gaining that support.

HARLEY-DAVIDSON

The Cambia Health Solutions and Allstate Insurance cases describe the initiation, design, and early dynamics of the agility transformation process. Their change strategies were guided by the agility principles outlined in this book, but their ultimate success is still to be determined. Now we look back at a complete transformation and its performance consequences. The Harley-Davidson (H-D) transformation was comprehensive and addressed setting the strategy, fixing the foundation, and building the routines over a period of about ten years. The explicit attention to the ITSS principle has produced an agile organization with sustained performance.

Harley-Davidson is one of a handful of companies we found that made the transition to high performer in this thirty-year period (Exhibit 5.1). But in 1980, H-D was as good as dead. Corporate parent American Machinery and Foundry (AMF) had put them up for sale and found no takers. Japanese competition had stolen a march on America's last

EXHIBIT 5.1.   *Auto Industry Performance*

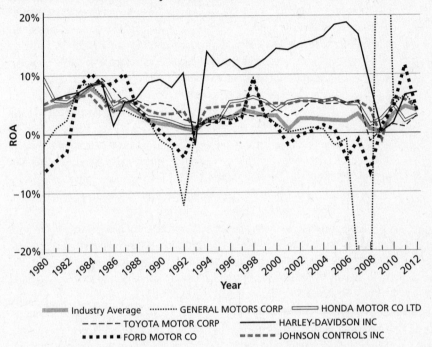

Industry Average   ·········· GENERAL MOTORS CORP   ⇒ HONDA MOTOR CO LTD
– – – – – TOYOTA MOTOR CORP   ——— HARLEY-DAVIDSON INC
■ ■ ■ ■ ■ ■ FORD MOTOR CO   ■ – ■ – ■ – JOHNSON CONTROLS INC

domestic motorcycle brand and opened up entirely new markets of com-
muter and recreational users. In 1981, Vaughn Beals and twelve other
H-D executives took the company private in a leveraged buyout. In a
desperate bid for survival, they shrank the company by one-third and
rapidly implemented a number of Toyota production system techniques
to improve product quality, which was terrible, and reduce costs. In
1982, H-D shipped 32,400 units. In 1983, they successfully petitioned
the Reagan administration for the "Harley Tariff" on imported motorcycles over 700cc to give them some breathing room. The year 1983
also saw the formation of the Harley Owners Group (HOG), a stroke of
marketing genius that created the largest factory-sponsored club of its
kind and became the carrier vehicle for direct communications between
H-D and its customers.

When Rich Teerlink took over from Vaughn Beals as head of
Harley-Davidson in 1987, he inherited a company that had been rescued
from the brink through a strong form of command-and-control
management that was necessary at the time. Going forward, Teerlink
wondered if he could produce high levels of performance in the absence
of a crisis through the commitment of employees rather than their
compliance with orders from the top.

Over the next decade, Teerlink and his senior management team engineered a complete transformation of Harley-Davidson to a model of shared leadership and accountability based on good management principles; transparent, integrated performance management; continuous improvement; learning and development; and organization agility. It was tough sledding that proceeded in fits and starts because H-D managers and employees were asked to go from a "Tell me what you want me to do" to a "Given where we're going, I'll figure out what's best to do" style of managing.

H-D's transformation attended to both aspects of strategy: identity and intent. Teerlink and his most senior managers, Tom Gelb, VP of manufacturing, and John Campbell, VP of human resources, began by codifying key aspects of Harley-Davidson's identity through the "Joint Vision Process." Initially, it involved bringing together the top 130 H-D managers for a three-day off-site to hammer out a desired future state for the company. Since its founding, Harley-Davidson had had nothing that resembled a vision, mission statement, or strategy. The management team started at the top, building a corporate identity under an "umbrella" of values, issues to be addressed, stakeholders to be served, and the long-term vision for the company. The corporate values were simple, forthright, and memorable: Tell the truth; be fair; keep your promises; respect the individual; encourage intellectual curiosity. Along the way, a new identity for Harley-Davidson evolved based on the company vision: "We fulfill dreams inspired by the many roads of the world by providing remarkable motorcycles and extraordinary customer experiences. We fuel the passion for freedom in our customers to express their own identity."

The corporate turnaround and migration toward a more agile organization was anchored in a strategy that emphasized quality improvement, operational efficiency, and customer satisfaction. At the same time, Harley-Davidson had to make some explicit choices about what business it was in. In 1986, its portfolio consisted of the heavyweight motorcycle business; the financial services business, through Harley-Davidson Financial Services (HDFS); and the luxury motorhome business, a result of their acquisition of Holiday Rambler. Through the lens of its vision and desired identity, it became apparent that Holiday Rambler was an inconsistent distraction that H-D eventually divested in 1995.

Harley's strategy also called for growth, and in 1991 they developed a plan to produce and ship a hundred thousand units by the end of 1996, a 208 percent increase over 1982. This required a complete restructuring of their manufacturing and product development operations. They worked with their two unions to restructure the factories in Milwaukee, Wisconsin, and York, Pennsylvania. They were able to build on their experience with the Toyota Production System to engage union leadership and factory employees on the need to change, motivated by the carrots of sales growth and gain sharing of profits.

The Joint Vision Process was eventually linked to other initiatives aimed at fixing the foundation of good management practices and building agile routines. In 1988, Teerlink and his team began looking hard at planning and performance management, which they called the Business Process. They built an integrated, cascading management system that provided line of sight from the most senior executive to the factory floor worker. Individuals developed personal goals as part of the Performance Effectiveness Process (PEP), which was incorporated into appraisals and variable compensation. Employees assumed personal accountability for their goals and their contribution toward achievement of their work unit plans. Through the Business Process, the activities of individuals were tagged and tied to the overall objectives of the company. Leadership and accountability were distributed throughout the organization. Said Teerlink at the time, "I believe fundamentally that people should have the opportunity to influence their lives and their workplace."

With the establishment of HOG in 1983, H-D had a good start on effective perceiving and testing routines. Everyone at Harley-Davidson touches the customer. Employees from the CEO on down ride with customers, attend HOG rallies, and participate in sponsored musical and sporting events. There is constant formal and informal contact with H-D dealer and supplier networks. As part of a product development effort for the next generation of cruising motorcycles, called Project Rushmore, the marketing team logged over a thousand hours of riding with customers to capture their emerging requirements and test particular concepts.

All these inputs get communicated to decision makers so that they can be interpreted and translated into action. Agile organizations such as H-D have shallow hierarchies, open communication links both vertically and horizontally, and an absence of gatekeepers who would impede or filter information flow to executives. Once communicated, environmental signals are interpreted in the context of the vision and strategic intent, competitive industry dynamics, and organizational capabilities. For example, given the high value placed on lifestyle and customization, customers can interact directly with company marketing and product development through H-D1, Harley's "factory custom" design web page.

The HOG and dealer connections provide inputs for changes, but these need to be critically reviewed for viability. At H-D, "tests" include marketing programs; model customizations; new motorcycle models, engines, and styling; new manufacturing methods; new ways of working; and new markets. To run these tests, H-D builds in slack resources to drive flexibility and innovation where it is needed most. One way H-D builds in slack is through its model of shared leadership and account-ability that allows managers to manage, not micromanage. This slack comes at a cost, but it is a deliberate investment that allows agile orga-nizations to rapidly deploy capable resources on opportunities without jeopardizing day-to-day operations. These resources, in the form of people, time, and assets, also play an important role in capturing and disseminating learning that the organization can use later.

Slack resources represent a deliberate investment that allows agile organizations to rapidly deploy capable resources on opportunities without jeopar-dizing day-to-day operations.

Under Teerlink, Harley-Davidson ran a number of programs and events to teach individuals and the organization how to learn, reflecting the company's "encourage intellectual curiosity" value. From 1989 through 1991, they ran a series of Awareness Expansion (AE) work-shops with managers to stimulate new ways of thinking. These sessions forced managers to consider alternative ways of managing and motivat-ing, controlling, and empowering the organization. This was new and frustrating; managers were heard to say, "Why doesn't Rich just tell us what he wants?" The objective, however, was to teach managers to learn from each other and be willing to draw their own conclusions.

In 1991, H-D created the Harley-Davidson Leadership Institute to centralize the various training and development programs going on around the company. In 1992, they entered into a long-term relationship with Peter Senge's Organizational Learning Center (OLC) at MIT. Also in 1992, they formed the Harley-Davidson University (HDU) to train and develop dealers in business management, customer service, and personal skills. By 2000, HDU could boast 1,800 paying dealers and staff enrolled in twenty-three courses. Individual and organiza-tional learning became an integral part of working at H-D.

For example, H-D adopted the military practice of After Action Reviews (AAR Process) to analyze both successes and failures. The closed-loop logic of plan-do-check-act applies to agility as much as to any other capability or business process. Capturing the lessons of the perceiving and testing stages is a critical element of building agility. It is also an important part of maintaining the currency of the organizations' strategy, business model, and capability set.

By the time Rich Teerlink retired in 1999, he had transformed Harley-Davidson from an inward-looking, marginal, command-and-control organization to an agile, dynamic market leader permeated with shared leadership and accountability. Contact with the environment is direct and pervasive. Information flows freely across an organic structure that mirrors major process flows. Curiosity, experimentation, and direct action are explicitly encouraged and rewarded. But it is a controlled chaos, held together by the centripetal forces of a strong identity, shared values, and the Business Process.

The transformation at H-D was comprehensive; it touched on strategy, good management, and agility routines. As a result of this comprehensive ITSS approach, the elements of H-D's design and their agility routines form a self-reinforcing whole that maintains its ability to adapt and keeps the organization open to learning.

The financial crisis and recession of 2008–2009 hit Harley-Davidson particularly hard. Sales of recreational luxury goods fell precipitously. HDFS was saddled with a large number of nonperforming loans, as heavily indebted consumers found themselves strapped for cash and their mortgages under water. In response, in 2009 H-D embarked on an operational restructuring of its business and manufacturing operations to reduce costs, increase flexibility, and build in surge capacity. By 2012, the project had delivered $280 million in actual cost savings against a 2008 baseline. They also embarked on an ambitious, integrated program to deliver a true "mass customization" capability. This involved standardizing and streamlining the product development process, enabling a wide variety of customization options via dealers and the web, and completely restructuring their manufacturing process to produce any custom version of any bike in any plant on any day. They engaged their unionized workforce to dramatically change work rules and moved from sixty-two job classifications to five. They have reorganized and scaled down their manufacturing footprint and restructured their supply base. When completed, H-D will have a customer-driven "pull" system that will increase flexibility, reduce inventory, and raise already high customer satisfaction levels.

One of the most difficult lessons for H-D has been keeping its strategic breadth aligned to its identity. H-D's traditional heavyweight touring and cruising products are large-displacement motorcycles with windshields, fairings, saddlebags, upright seating, and custom accessories. They are designed for comfortable cruising on the open road.

In 1993, even as they were recognizing the misfit of the Holiday Rambler business, H-D acquired a minority stake in Buell, a high-performance sport bike developed by an ex-Harley engineer. H-D then sold Buell motorcycles, "powered by Harley-Davidson" engines, through Harley dealerships. Sport bikes are an entirely different category, stripped down to save weight and more attuned for racing. While Harley-Davidsons had raced successfully since the company's inception in 1903, sport bikes, like luxury motor homes, were inconsistent with their brand image. Nevertheless, in 1998 H-D acquired a majority stake in Buell. Sales volumes were low, and margins were lower than on the touring and cruising bikes.

As part of its plans for expansion into Europe, in 2008 H-D announced an agreement to purchase MV Augusta for $109 million. MV Augusta is a storied Italian brand that is to motorcycles what Ferrari is to cars. Originally founded by an Italian count with a passion for racing, MV Augusta produces high-technology works of motorcycle art in small quantities that belong on the track or in museums. As with Buell, the product and customer segments are entirely different from those of traditional H-D. There was a historical connection, however: Caviga, the parent company of MV Augusta, started production in 1978 in a disused AMF Harley-Davidson factory.

But in October 2009, in an abrupt turnaround, H-D announced that it would sell MV Augusta back to Claudio Castiglione, at what turned out to be a considerable loss. At the same time, they discontinued the Buell line. Keith Wandell, Harley-Davidson's new CEO, had determined that neither MV Augusta nor Buell were a fit with the company's identity and strategy.

Most recently, the entire agility system of strategizing, perceiving, testing, and implementing came together in Harley-Davidson's first new motorcycle family in fourteen years, "The Street." This entry-level Harley comes in 500cc and 750cc engine configurations and is aimed at a new generation of young urban riders. Shown at the 2013 Geneva Motor Show, The Street was launching in 2014 simultaneously in the United States, Europe, and Asia. Unlike previous "entry" Harleys, it is not an outsourced machine that has been rebadged. It is entirely true to the Harley image: V-twin engine, long wheelbase, upright seating, and customization options. This new market should add significantly to the 260,000 motorcycles Harley-Davidson shipped in 2013.

CONCLUSION

Becoming agile takes time, effort, resources, patience, and a great managerial willingness to employ trial and error. In a sense, one learns agility while trying to implement it. No two organizations we have seen did it the same way, but they had the same inchoate vision of how they wanted to be more flexible, nimble, dynamic, or fast. The complete transformation at Harley-Davidson took almost a decade. Cambia and Allstate are both just a few years in but already demonstrating progress and improved performance. We will monitor their progress with interest.

AFTERWORD

Some Reflections on Agility

The great thing in the world is not so much where
we stand as in what direction we are moving.

—OLIVER WENDELL HOLMES

Organizations, like people, are born, thrive, suffer, and die. With any luck, there is more thriving than suffering, but the truth is that the vast majority of organizations do not last more than five years.[1] Competitive environments can be hostile places, and globalization has made them even more so. Since 1980, the starting point for our financial data, there have been tremendous changes in the competitive environment of every industry, and every indicator suggests that the pace of change is increasing.

The population ecology school of business research, introduced in Chapter Two, has analyzed rich databases to understand the dynamics of organizations in their environments over time. The Darwinian processes of variation, selection, and retention act on members of the population, rewarding those with the best environmental fit and eliminating those without. Variations come in the form of new organizations, because most existing organizations are unable to adapt at the pace required to keep up with environmental changes. Although population ecology offers a powerful description of how industries evolve, it offers little prescriptive insight or solace to managers. The environment determines whether your firm lives or dies.

A strategic choice or resource-based view of the firm, however, does allow organizations to change and adapt to dynamic environments, albeit at considerable risk. Practical people, such as business managers, know that corporations can and do change all the time, either incrementally (continuous improvement) or dramatically (restructuring). Most large corporations repeat a success formula until it no longer works, and only then do they seek and implement an alternative. In our language, they "thrash."

In every industry we examined, there was a handful of large companies that had internalized the environmental forces of variation, selection, and retention and put them to productive use. We observed that their evolution was more like that described not by Darwin, but by Lamarck, in that their variations were chosen, not random.[2] They were not victims of their initial endowments or their fates. They anticipated, they acted, and somehow they made better bets than their peers.

Running a large, complex organization is hard; changing an organization is difficult and fraught with risk. Simultaneously running and changing a business seems to be an overwhelming endeavor that depends on a delicate balance of initiative and control. Agility is a very advanced organizational capability that delivers that balance through a system of routines that can modify the organization's capabilities and management practices when and where it provides a competitive advantage.

Researchers and consultants like us are constantly looking for the new insights, frameworks, or tools that will give companies a performance edge. Agility seems to deliver such a competitive advantage. But we also know that despite decades of organizational research and thousands of MBA graduates, most organizations do not effectively apply proven practices of sound management.[3] Worse yet, the fundamentals of management still seem to be missing in industry.

A 2013 Gallup poll reinforced the findings of a similar 2007 poll: only about 30 percent of employed Americans are actively engaged at work. More than half of the workforce merely shows up, and 20 percent are actively disengaged, sabotaging the performance of their employers. The survey reveals that the root cause is mismanagement. Yet the means by which organizations can engage workers have been well understood for over fifty years.

The survey also shows that good management pays off. Companies ranked in the top quartile of employee engagement are 22 percent more profitable than companies ranked in the bottom quartile. This is another reason why we spent so much time on "good management." These survey results raise the question, "Why don't rational managers apply known best practices?"

Agility is the management equivalent of football's "West Coast offense." A team that cannot block and tackle is incapable of managing the dynamism of variable blocking assignments and optional receiver routes that depend on accurately reading the defense. Agility is for only those companies that have already mastered the basics.

Agility allows an organization to develop and pursue options that it would not otherwise have. The perceiving routine stimulates management to create responses to environmental signals that potentially generate value. Some of these are selected for testing and eventually retained through implementation. These responses can be used for good or ill. There is nothing inherently moral or ethical about the agility capability. We did not study it directly, but the Camorra crime syndicate of Naples may be as agile as ExxonMobil, Harley-Davidson, or Campbell's. The organizational capability to respond to environmental threats or opportunities could as easily include rent-seeking as it could sustainable development. Agility could result in the launch of a devastating price war that changes the competitive landscape—or the introduction of free on-site day care to help the retention of a valued workforce.

Our focus up to this point has been on explaining agility. In these final pages, we want to explore the positive potential of agility. For example, in describing sustained performance and providing examples of how organizations are manifesting agility in their designs, we suspect that agility may represent a piece of the solution to sustainability. In describing what we learned about how organizations are making the transformation to agility, we believe that agility may represent a way to reinvigorate the field of organization development. Other implications—for human resource management, government and regulatory policy, or globalization—can and should be explored as well.

AGILITY AND SUSTAINABILITY

One way organizations seek to improve their performance is by influencing the environment itself. Competitors are the most salient feature of a business environment, but regulation often plays a crucial role. In 2000, over twelve thousand registered lobbying organizations spent $1.57 billion to influence federal legislation. By 2010, that figure had more than doubled to $3.55 billion. In 2013, the top two industry sectors, finance and health, spent a combined $960 million on federal lobbying. This should come as no surprise as the regulations implementing the Dodd-Frank Wall Street Reform and Consumer Protection Act and the Patient Protection and Affordable Care Act (Obamacare) were being written. As a result, many of the safeguards designed to prevent a repeat of the 2007 financial crisis have been severely diluted. Financial institutions that were "too big to fail" in 2007 are even larger in 2013, and their capital requirements have not been appreciably raised. Medicare and Medicaid are enjoined from using their purchasing power to lower the prices of prescription drugs. Large industry players are paid to preserve an environment that gave them an advantage. Economists call this "regulatory capture." It is one of many ways to tilt the playing field in one's favor.

Suppose, however, that an agile organization chose not to exploit or ravage its environment, but to adopt a more complex objective function of "sustainable effectiveness" through pursuit of a triple bottom line of economic, environmental, and social outcomes.[4] Such an objective function not only would produce positive economic, social, and environmental outcomes but would do so over time. We believe that the agility capability would significantly improve that firm's chances of success in this risky endeavor through its ability to make better bets and rapidly implement chosen adaptations.

Management in such an enterprise would need to be confident that the short- and long-term economic advantages associated with consuming less energy, using fewer inputs, polluting less, reducing their carbon footprint, paying living wages, or any number of actions associated with sustainability would exceed the disadvantages. To accelerate implementation and gain organizational commitment, they would embed sustainability in their strategic intent and, ultimately, in their identity, as Nokia; Gap, Inc.; and Patagonia have done. Real resources would then be applied to perceiving, testing, and implementing processes and technologies to deliver on the promise. Such moves would go well beyond the marketing hype many companies adopt to project an image of sustainability.

Should our hypothetical company succeed, it might embark on some regulatory capture of its own. The investments in sustainability would provide a competitive advantage. It could lobby for regulations that address environmental or social issues and that, if enacted, would put its competitors at a comparative disadvantage. An industry leader in sustainability could initiate a virtuous cycle of societal improvement.

Until industrial organizations, consumers, and governments collectively choose to address these issues, ocean temperatures and sea levels will continue to rise, glaciers will retreat, species will go extinct at abnormal rates, and economic inequality will increase. These are the realities individuals and organizations must address. Organizations that possess agility will accept the evidence that these drivers of potential catastrophe are real, build these notions into their strategic scenarios, and put plans into place to deal with the unthinkable when it occurs. Agile and sustainable organizations are more likely to survive, while the rest will suffer the consequences of their denial.

AGILITY AND ORGANIZATION DEVELOPMENT

In the economic and social wakes of World War II, the field of organization development (OD) emerged, grew, and flourished. It was OD that helped organizations make the initial shift from command-and-control-oriented bureaucracies to high-involvement organizations.[5] Practitioners of organization development had a clear and shared purpose and a set of strategies and practices that leveraged participation and involvement to improve effectiveness and *develop* organizations.[6] Using behavioral science knowledge, OD practitioners *intervened* in the ongoing work streams and norms of operations.

Following Douglas McGregor's lead, they saw people's motivations, emotions, and the quality of their interpersonal relationships as legitimate sources of organization effectiveness. Moreover, OD held that understanding these human processes could lead to more effective change processes. Typical OD change processes transferred behavioral and social sciences skills and knowledge to the client system—through assessment, reflection, and participation—thereby building the capacity to manage change in the future. They sought to integrate technical and social knowledge to create effective, adaptable organizations.[7] In the mid-1960s and early 1970s, new work and organization designs, built on these principles, resulted in impressive results in organizations as diverse as Procter & Gamble, TRW, and Volvo, and most of the early, traditional OD innovations—including climate and engagement surveys, team building, and change management—have been institutionalized in business practice.

But somewhere along the line, the field of OD lost its way, and corporate investment in and support for it has dwindled. Although most large organizations have established OD functions, they are typically small and most are not major players in their organizations.

From our perspective, OD wasn't agile. It didn't adapt to new realities, clung too closely to the things it already knew, and failed to pursue the integration of human potential and operational effectiveness. The field generally advocates a too narrow and linear view of how change occurs, a view that doesn't map to the realities of change in most organizations. The unfreezing-moving-refreezing model and other linear approaches to change management lead executives and others to believe that "change will be over." Too many processes focused on "making change stick" have been perverted into "making change stop."

There is a strong division among OD practitioners and researchers regarding the field's purpose. One camp holds that OD has become too corporate, co-opted by organizational power holders, and too focused on organization effectiveness over human potential. The other camp feels just the opposite: they believe that OD has become overly enamored with the emotional side of change and prioritizes social over economic effectiveness.

Both of these views can be seen in practice today. On the one hand, some OD practitioners overuse the strengths of the approach. The attention to process and human potential has become the objective rather than the strategy for achieving organizational adaptability. Team building, process consultation, conflict management, coaching, and survey feedback—done without reference to or integration with strategy and structure—suboptimize OD's potential. On the other hand, some practitioners, under the umbrella of OD, have become project managers. They blindly apply the latest tool to develop a change playbook that can be rolled out, to design a process for dealing with resistance, or to construct the right set of talking points so that leaders communicate consistently. These narrow and fragmented perspectives marginalize OD's contributions in organizations, limit its potential, and put its practitioners in a defensive posture.[8]

Agile organizations need an effective OD function. But rather than focusing primarily on people or tools, it should be asking, "What's the next, best, right thing that needs to be done to make this *organization* more effective?" And in this regard, OD lacks any model to accompany and complement its process strengths. Agility, and more specifically the Agility Pyramid, represents one potential model. Developing organizations that can make timely, effective, and sustained changes gives OD an opportunity to reengage with its original objectives: transferring to organization members the knowledge and skill needed to strategize, perceive, test, and implement the processes, systems, structures, and strategies that ensure sustained performance.

OD practitioners can help their organizations become more agile by learning the ways of agility. First, the Agility Pyramid represents a new and effective diagnostic framework with change at its core. Diagnosis is a hallmark feature of OD, and the processes associated with understanding the organization's agility routines allow the organization to understand its strengths and weaknesses. Second, the Agility Pyramid implies a developmental sequence and change strategy. At the base of the pyramid are the good management practices—planning, organizing, directing, and controlling—that every organization engages in. OD is uniquely suited to facilitate the transformation to agility by helping organizations build more flexible and sophisticated management processes, and it can help organizations develop and build the capability sets that will differentiate them from competitors. Capability development has been a passing fancy in OD; it must become a central focus of practice.

Finally, OD practitioners need to become fluent in the language and design of agile routines. The categories of change from Chapter Five—setting the strategy, fixing the foundation, and building the agility routines—can be used to support transformation. Designing change processes and interventions is OD's strength, and OD practitioners need to continue relying on their understanding of process. Appreciating the role of motivation, emotion, and interpersonal relationships and their contribution to both effectiveness and change remains a sadly missing component in the thinking of too many organizations and their leaders. However, the examples of transformation in Chapter Five were based on an understanding of organization design principles that are not utilized or known by most OD practitioners. For OD to capture its full potential and contribute to the development of continually effective organizations, OD practitioners must devote themselves to developing the skills and knowledge related to the principles and frameworks of strategy, organization design, and capabilities. By returning to its original purpose—the transfer of knowledge and skill to client systems so they possess the capability to change themselves—and by returning to its original methods—the integration of human process and organization design—OD can be a relevant and important contributor to agility.

CONCLUSION

Agility is one of today's "hot topics" among researchers, executives, and consultants. This is not likely to change soon. Environments, technologies, markets, and regulations are not going to stop changing, so the ability to adapt quickly and effectively will remain an important capability. We have tried, in this book, to describe the elements and routines of agility and to demonstrate that such a capability is an important source of sustained performance, and, in this Afterword, to demonstrate that such a framework might perhaps be a source of sustainability and organization development.

NOTES

PREFACE

1. A. M. Wilson, J. C. Lowe, et al., "Locomotion dynamics of hunting in wild cheetahs." *Nature*, 498 (2013, June 13): 185–189.

CHAPTER 1

1. C. I. Stubbart and M. B. Knight, "The case of the disappearing firms: Empirical evidence and implications." *Journal of Organizational Behavior*, 27(1) (2006): 79–100.

2. R. Foster and S. Kaplan, *Creative destruction: Why companies that are built to last underperform the market—And how to successfully transform them* (New York: Random House, 2011).

3. R. Burgman and M. Van Clieaf, "Total shareholder return (TSR) and management performance: A performance metric appropriately used, or mostly abused?" *Rotman International Journal of Pension Management*, 5(2) (2012): 26–33.

4. J. Collins and J. Porras, *Built to last* (New York: HarperCollins, 1994); W. Joyce, N. Nohria, and B. Roberson, *What really works: The 4+2 formula for sustained business success* (New York: HarperCollins, 2003).

5. A. McGahan, "Competition, strategy, and business performance." *California Management Review* 41(3) (1999): 74–101; A. M. McGahan, "The performance of US corporations: 1981–1994." *Journal of Industrial Economics*, 47(4) (1999): 373–398; A. M. McGahan and M. E. Porter, "What do we know about variance in accounting profitability?" *Management Science*, 48(7) (2002): 834–851.

6. A few comments on our sample and benchmarks are warranted. First, similar to McGahan, we used the largest firms in the industry, but "large" was determined qualitatively by looking for an inflection point in a "scree plot" of organizations ranked by revenues and assets. The logic of this

choice was that it is the other large firms that are likely to be viewed as competitors. Second, there will always be some arbitrariness in establishing industry boundaries when those boundaries are constantly in flux. When does HP change from a small instruments business to a computer company? Does Apple belong in the computer industry or the telecom instrument business? Third, for the industry averages we also used the mean for all existing firms in the industry for a particular year. This "population" mean—all firms offering close substitutes—allowed us to test the robustness of our findings. In all cases, the population mean—usually by virtue of many small firms that would eventually fail—proved to be a very easy benchmark to beat. The sample's mean was the real test of competitiveness and performance.

7. S. Winter, "Understanding dynamic capabilities." *Strategic Management Journal*, 24(10) (2003): 991–995.

8. H. Simon, *Administrative behavior* (New York: Macmillan, 1947).

9. M. Hannan and J. Freeman, "The population ecology of organizations." *American Journal of Sociology*, 82 (1977): 929–964; H. Aldrich, *Organizations evolving* (London: SAGE Publications, 1999).

10. C. Christensen, *The innovator's dilemma: When new technologies cause great firms to fail* (Cambridge: Harvard Business School Press, 1997).

11. Deloitte Center for the Edge, Measuring the forces of long-term change (2011), http://www.deloitte.com/assets/Dcom-UnitedStates/Local%20 Assets/Documents/TMT_us_tmt/us_tmt_shiftindex_revised_120512.pdf, last accessed on August 20, 2013; R. Wiggins and T. Ruefli, "Schumpeter's ghost: Is hypercompetition making the best of times shorter?" *Strategic Management Journal*, 26 (2005): 887–911.

12. R. D'Aveni, *Hypercompetition* (New York: Free Press, 1994).

13. T. Peters and R. Waterman, *In search of excellence: Lessons from America's best-run companies* (New York: HarperCollins, 2004).

14. J. Collins, *Good to great: Why some companies make the leap…and others don't* (New York: HarperCollins (2001); J. Collins and J. Porras, *Built to last: Successful habits of visionary companies* (New York: HarperCollins, 2004).

15. B. Niendorf and K. Beck, "Good to great or just good?" *Academy of Management Perspectives*, 22(4) (2008): 13–20; B. Resnick and T. Smunt, "From good to great to…" *Academy of Management Perspectives*, 22(4) (2008): 6–12.

16. J. Child, "Organizational structure, environment and performance: The role of strategic choice." *Sociology*, 6 (1972): 1–22; M. Beer and R. Eisenstat, "Developing an organization capable of implementing strategy and learning." *Human Relations*, 49 (1996): 597–619; D. J. Teece, G. Pisano, and A. Shuen, "Dynamic capabilities and strategic management." *Strategic Management Journal*, 18(7) (1991): 509–533.

17. M. Tushman and C. O'Reilly, "Ambidextrous organizations: Managing evolutionary and revolutionary change." *California Management Review*, 38 (1996): 8–30; H. Volberda, *Building the flexible firm: How to remain competitive* (New York: Oxford University Press, 1998); D. Sull, *The upside of turbulence* (New York: Harper Business, 2008); E. E. Lawler and C. Worley, *Built to change* (San Francisco: Jossey-Bass, 2006); S. Haeckel, *Adaptive enterprise: Creating and leading sense-and-respond organizations* (Boston: Harvard Business School Press, 1999).

18. E. Romanelli and M. Tushman, "Organizational transformation as punctuated equilibrium: An empirical test." *Academy of Management Journal*, 37 (1994): 1141–1166; T. Lant and S. Mezias, "An organizational learning model of convergence and reorientation." *Organization Science*, 3 (1992): 47–71.

CHAPTER 2

1. G. Vickers, *Freedom in a rocking boat* (Middlesex, UK: Penguin Books, 1970).

2. I. Barreto, "Dynamic capabilities: A review of past research and an agenda for the future." *Journal of Management*, 36(1) (2010): 256–280.

3. H. Koontz and C. O'Donnell, *Principles of management* (3rd ed.) (New York: McGraw-Hill, 1964).

4. B. Wernerfelt, "A resource-based view of the firm." *Strategic Management Journal*, 5(2) (1984): 171–180; J. Barney, "Resource-based theories of competitive advantage: A ten-year retrospective on the resource-based view." *Journal of Management*, 27(6) (2001): 643–650.

5. J. Galbraith, *Designing organizations* (San Francisco: Jossey-Bass, 2002); S. Mohrman and C. Worley, "Dealing with rough times: A capabilities development approach to surviving and thriving." *Human Resource Management*, 48(3) (2009): 433–445.

6. P. Leinwand and C. Mainardi, *The essential advantage* (Cambridge: Harvard University Press, 2010).

7. B. Wernerfelt. "A resource-based view of the firm." *Strategic Management Journal*, 5 (1984): 171–180; M. Peteraf, "The cornerstones of competitive advantage: a resource-based view." *Strategic Management Journal*, 14(3) (1993): 179–191.

8. R. Nelson and S. Winter, *An evolutionary theory of economic change* (Cambridge, MA: Harvard University Press, 1982).

9. S. G. Winter, "The satisficing principle in capability learning." *Strategic Management Journal*, 21 (Oct/Nov 2000): 983.

10. I. Barreto, "Dynamic capabilities: A review of past research and an agenda for the future." *Journal of Management*, 36(1) (2010): 271.

11. R. D'Aveni, G. Dagnino, and K. Smith, "The age of temporary advantage." *Strategic Management Journal*, 31(3) (2010): 1371–1385.

12. M. Hannan and J. Freeman, "The population ecology of organizations." *American Journal of Sociology*, 82(5) (1977): 929–964; M. Hannan and J. Freeman, *Organizational ecology* (Boston: Harvard University Press, 1989); G. Carroll and M. Hannan (Eds.), *Organizations in industry: Strategy, structure, & selection* (New York: Oxford University Press, 1995).

13. M. Hannan and J. Freeman, "Structural inertia and organizational change." *American Sociological Review*, 49(2) (1984): 151.

14. J. O'Toole and W. Bennis, "What's needed next: A culture of candor." *Harvard Business Review*, 87(6) (2009): 54.

15. J. Collins and J. Porras, *Built to last* (New York: HarperCollins, 1994); D. Lavie, U. Stettner, and M. Tushman, "Exploration and exploitation within and across organizations." *The Academy of Management Annals*, 4(1) (2010): 109–155.

16. The materials for this case description come from a variety of sources, including J. Pfeffer, K. Thiry, and DaVita, *Leadership challenges in building and growing a great company* (Stanford, CA: Stanford Graduate School of Business, 2006); articles, website information, and interviews with company teammates.

17. C. Snow, "Renal-Care Biggies Plan Merger." *Modern Healthcare*, 27(47) (1997): 20.

18. *Los Angeles Business Journal*, October 23, 2000.

19. Originally there were six values, but over the years a seventh value, "fun," was added by another election.

20. M. Feldman and B. Pentland, "Reconceptualizing organizational routines as a source of flexibility and change." *Administrative Science Quarterly*, 48(1) (2003): 94–118.

21. C. Argyris, "Double loop learning in organizations." *Harvard Business Review*, 55(5) (1977): 115–125.

22. For a complementary view, see R. Whittington, A. Pettigrew, S. Peck, E. Fenton, and M. Conyon, "Change and complementarities in the new competitive landscape: A European panel study, 1992–1996." *Organization Science*, 10 (1999): 583–600.

23. To be clear, possessing a routine means that the organization's score on, say, testing is higher than average for all sample firms. We believe this sets a relatively high bar, in that while the sample of firms is composed of mostly thrashers and underperformers, there is a higher percentage of outperforming firms than naturally found in the population. Just being "above average" in three out of four routines is a difficult achievement.

24. The thresholds for our assessment ratings were as follows. To be considered significantly above average, a company's score on any of the agility routines had to be more than two standard deviations above the mean. To be moderately above average, scores had to be more than one standard deviation above the mean, and to be slightly above average, scores had to be above the mean.

CHAPTER 3

1. P. Dvorak, "Experts have a message for managers: Shake it up." *Wall Street Journal*, June 6, 2008, B8.

2. K. Andrews, *The concept of corporate strategy* (Homewood, IL: Dow Jones-Irwin, 1971), 52–53.

3. D. A. Whetten, "Albert and Whetten revisited: Strengthening the concept of organizational identity." *Journal of Management Inquiry*, 15(3) (2006): 219–234; M. J. Hatch and M. Schultz, "The dynamics of organizational identity." *Human Relations*, 55(8) (2002): 989–1018.

4. B. Hindo, "At 3M, a struggle between efficiency and creativity." *Business Week*, 11 (2007): 8–14.

5. M. Porter, "What is strategy?" *Harvard Business Review*, November-December 1996.

6. G. Willigan, *Nokia: Values that make a company global* (Alexandria, VA: Society for Human Resource Management, 2009).

7. I first heard this clever phrase from Dr. Arif Kachra when he was on the faculty at Pepperdine University.

8. W. Cohen and D. Levinthal, "Absorptive capacity: A new perspective on learning and innovation." *Administrative Science Quarterly*, 35(1) (1990): 128–152.

9. Cohen and Levinthal, "Absorptive capacity: A new perspective," 136.

10. Ibid.; S. Zahra and G. George, "Absorptive capacity: A review, reconceptualization, and extension." *Academy of Management Review*, 27(2) (2002): 185–203; R. Burgelman, "Intraorganizational ecology of strategy making and organizational adaptation: Theory and field research." *Organization Science*, 2(3) (1991): 239–262.

11. S. Raisch, J. Birkinshaw, G. Probst, and M. L. Tushman, "Organizational ambidexterity: Balancing exploitation and exploration for sustained performance." *Organization Science*, 20(4) (2009): 685–695; D. Lavie, U. Stettner, and M. Tushman, "Exploration and exploitation within and across organizations," *Academy of Management Annals*, 4 (2010): 109–155.

12. Cohen and Levinthal, "Absorptive capacity: A new perspective," 132.

13. H. Chesbrough, *Open innovation: The new imperative for creating and profiting from technology* (Boston: Harvard Business School Press, 2003).

14. J. O'Toole and W. Bennis, "What's needed next: A culture of candor." *Harvard Business Review*, 87(6) (2009): 54; M. Beer. *High commitment high performance: How to build a resilient organization for sustained advantage* (San Francisco: Jossey-Bass, 2009).

15. Burgelman, "Intraorganizational ecology," 252.

16. J. Ewing, "Nokia: Bring on the employee rants." *BusinessWeek* (2009, June 22): 50.

17. M. Lindgren and H. Bandhold, *Scenario planning: The link between future and strategy* (New York: Palgrave Macmillan, 2002); T. Chermack, *Scenario planning in organizations* (San Francisco: Berrett-Koehler, 2011); P. Schwartz, *The art of the long view* (New York: Random House, 1996).

18. Cohen and Levinthal, "Absorptive capacity: A new perspective"; Zahra and George, "Absorptive capacity: A review, reconceptualization, and extension."

19. I. M. Cockburn, R. M. Henderson, and S. Stern, "Untangling the origins of competitive advantage." *Strategic Management Journal*, 21(10–11) (2000): 1123–1145.

20. The thresholds for our assessment ratings were as follows. To be considered significantly above average, a company's score on any of the agility routines had to be more than two standard deviations above the mean. To be moderately above average, scores had to be more than one standard deviation above the mean, and to be slightly above average, scores had to be above the mean.

CHAPTER 4

1. C. Worley and E. Lawler, "Building a change capability at Capital One Financial Services." *Organizational Dynamics*, 38 (2009): 245–251.

2. C. O'Reilly and M. Tushman, "Ambidexterity as a dynamic capability: Resolving the innovator's dilemma." In A. Brief and B. Staw (Eds.), *Research in organizational behavior*, vol. 28 (2008): 185–206; M. Farjoun, "Beyond dualism: Stability and change as a duality." *Academy of Management Review*, 35(2) (2010): 202–225; M. L. Tushman and E. Romanelli, "Organizational evolution: A metamorphosis model of convergence and reorientation." In L. L. Cummings and B. M. Staw (Eds.), *Research in organizational behavior* (vol. 7, pp. 71–222) (Greenwich, CT: JAI Press, 1985).

3. W. Coyne, "Building a tradition of innovation." United Kingdom Department of Trade and Industry Innovation Lecture, London, 1996. Cited in R. Garud, J. Gehman, and A. Kumaraswamy, "Complexity arrangements for sustained innovation: Lessons from 3M Corporation." *Organization Studies*, 32(6) (2011): 737–767.

4. Garud, Gehman, and Kumaraswamy, "Complexity arrangements for sustained innovation."

5. R. Boland and F. Collopy, *Managing as designing* (Palo Alto: Stanford Business Books, 2004).

6. R. Burgelman, "Intraorganizational ecology of strategy making and organizational adaptation: Theory and field research." *Organization Science*, 2(3) (1991): 239–262.

7. Zahra and George, "Absorptive capacity: A review, reconceptualization, and extension," 190.

8.   P. Anderson and M. Tushman, "Technological discontinuities and dominant designs: A cyclical model of technological change." *Administrative Science Quarterly*, 35 (1990): 604–633.

9.   Garud, Gehman, and Kumaraswamy, "Complexity arrangements," 739.

10.   M. Feldman and B. Pentland, "Reconceptualizing organizational routines as a source of flexibility and change." *Administrative Science Quarterly*, 48(1) (March 2003): 94–118.

11.   R. Garud, P. Tuertscher, and A. Van de Ven, "Perspectives on innovation processes." *Academy of Management Annals*, 7 (2013): 775–819.

12.   A. Hill, "Killing off projects is the hardest innovation." *Financial Times* (2013). Accessed October 10, 2013, http://www.ft.com/cms/s/0/c313c96a -965c-11e2-9ab2-00144feabdc0.html#axzz2hMEFqGBN.

13.   G. Cattani, "Preadaptation, firm heterogeneity, and technological performance: A study on the evolution of fiber optics, 1970–1995." *Organization Science*, 16(6) (2005): 563–580.

14.   Burgelman, "Intraorganizational ecology."

15.   Ibid., 251.

16.   L. Bossidy and R. Charan, *Execution* (New York: Crown Books, 2002).

17.   V. Govindarajan and C. Trimble, "Building breakthrough businesses within established organizations." *Harvard Business Review*, 83(5) (2005): 58–68.

18.   S. Anderson Forest, "Blockbuster CEO's days in court." *BusinessWeek* (2002, June 12). Accessed November 30, 2013, http://www.businessweek .com/bwdaily/dnflash/jun2002/nf20020618_5409.htm.

19.   I. Barreto, "Dynamic capabilities: A review of past research and an agenda for the future." *Journal of Management*, 36(1) (2010): 256–280.

20.   S. Brown and K. Eisenhardt, *Competing on the edge* (Cambridge: Harvard Business School Press, 1998).

21.   S. Martin, "Netflix service gets a TV makeover." *USA Today*, November 13, 2013. http://www.usatoday.com/story/tech/2013/11/13/netflix-service -gets-a-tv-makeover/3500353/.

CHAPTER 5

1.   R. Tenkasi, S. Mohrman, and A. Mohrman, "Accelerated learning during organizational transition." In S. Mohrman, J. Galbraith, E. Lawler, and

Associates (Eds.), *Tomorrow's organization* (San Francisco: Jossey-Bass, 1998).

2. That is, the organizational component of agility requires at least three strong routines. But if the organization's agility profile is strong strategizing, perceiving, and testing—we call this a "weak form" of agility— sustaining performance is difficult. Practically speaking, less than 2 percent of the firms in our sample had this profile.

3. J. R. Wells, "The Allstate Corporation." Harvard Business School case 9–708–485 (Cambridge, MA: Harvard Business School Press, 2008).

4. B. Bunker and B. Alban, *Large group interventions* (San Francisco: Jossey-Bass, 1997).

5. M. Weisbord, *Productive workplaces* (San Francisco: Jossey-Bass, 1987).

6. G. Vickers, *Freedom in a rocking boat* (Middlesex, UK: Penguin Books, 1970), 142.

AFTERWORD

1. C. I. Stubbart and M. B. Knight, "The case of the disappearing firms: Empirical evidence and implications." *Journal of Organizational Behavior*, 27(1) (2006): 79–100.

2. B. McKelvey, *Organizational systematics* (Los Angeles: University of California Press, 1982).

3. J. Pfeffer and R. Sutton, *The knowing-doing gap* (Boston: Harvard Business School Press, 1999).

4. S. A. Mohrman and A. B. Shani (Eds.), *Organizing for sustainable effectiveness*. Volume 1 of the Organizing for Sustainability Series (London: Emerald Press, 2011); E. Lawler and C. Worley, *Management reset* (San Francisco: Jossey-Bass, 2011); J. Elkington, "Partnerships from cannibals with forks: The triple bottom line of 21st-century business." *Environmental Quality Management*, 8(1) (1998): 37–51.

5. A. Kleiner, *The age of heretics* (New York: Doubleday, 1996).

6. T. Cummings and C. Worley, *Organization development and change* (10th ed.) (Mason, OH: Cengage Publishing, 2014).

7. S. Steers, "Problems in the measurement of organization effectiveness." *Administrative Science Quarterly*, 10 (1975): 546–558; J. Campbell, "On the nature of organizational effectiveness." In P. S. Goodman and J. M.

Pennings (Eds.), *New perspectives on organizational effectiveness* (San Francisco: Jossey-Bass, 1977).

8. D. Bradford and W. Burke (Eds.), *Reinventing organization development* (New York: Wiley, 2005); R. Marshak, *Covert processes at work* (San Francisco: Berrett-Koehler, 2006); C. Worley and A. Feyerherm, "Reflections on the future of organization development." *Journal of Applied Behavioral Science*, 39(1) (2003): 97–115.

ABOUT THE
AUTHORS

Christopher G. Worley (Ph.D., University of Southern California) is a senior research scientist at the Center for Effective Organizations (USC's Marshall School of Business) and professor of management in Pepperdine University's Master of Science in Organization Development (MSOD) program. Dr. Worley's most recent books, coauthored with Ed Lawler, are *Management Reset* and *Built to Change*. He also authored *Integrated Strategic Change*, and with Tom Cummings has coauthored six editions of *Organization Development and Change*, the leading textbook on organization development. His articles on agility and strategic organization design have appeared in the *Journal of Applied Behavioral Science*, *Strategy+Business*, *Journal of Organization Behavior*, *MIT Sloan Management Review*, and *Organizational Dynamics*. Together, he and his wife, Debbie, are learning to be empty nesters in their San Juan Capistrano, California, home.

Thomas Williams is a senior executive advisor with Booz & Company (formerly Booz Allen Hamilton). In twenty-six years of management consulting, he has worked with global Fortune 1000 firms on issues of strategy, organization, capability building, and operations in North America, Europe, and Asia. Since 1999, he has worked with the USC Center for Effective Organizations and the World Economic Forum on research projects involving organizational alignment and agility. He received his master's degree from the Yale School of Management and a bachelor's degree in economics from Lawrence University.

Edward E. Lawler III is Distinguished Professor of Business and director of the Center for Effective Organizations in the Marshall School of Business at the University of Southern California. He joined USC in 1978 and during 1979 founded and became director of the University's Center for Effective Organizations. He has consulted with over one hundred organizations on employee involvement, organizational change, and compensation and has been honored as a top contributor to the fields of organizational development, organizational behavior, corporate governance, and human resource management.

He is the author of over 350 articles and 45 books. His articles have appeared in leading academic journals as well as *Fortune*, *Harvard Business Review*, and leading newspapers including *USA Today* and the *Financial Times*. His books include *Rewarding Excellence* (2000), *Corporate Boards: New Strategies for Adding Value at the Top* (2001), *Organizing for High Performance* (2001), *Treat People Right* (2003), *Human Resources Business Process Outsourcing* (2004), *Built to Change* (2006), *America at Work* (2006), *The New American Workplace* (2006), *Talent: Making People Your Competitive Advantage* (2008), *Useful Research: Advancing Theory and Practice* (2011), *Management Reset: Organizing for Sustainable Effectiveness* (2011), and *Effective Human Resource Management: A Global Analysis* (2012). For more information, visit http://www.edwardlawler.com and http://ceo.usc.edu.

ACKNOWLEDGMENTS

First, acknowledgments must go to the companies who granted us the privilege of understanding their strategies, cultures, and organizations. The organizations described here are not perfect—no organization is—but they represent the vanguard of organization design.

Second, a number of friends and colleagues helped us along the way. Chris would like to thank Warren Bennis, Sue Mohrman, Rich Reynolds, Foster Mobley, and Tony Petrella for their support and for refining our thinking, assisting us in the research, and reading and commenting on various chapters in the book. To Debbie, my wife of thirty years, and my family, who know all too well how hard this journey has been, I am deeply humbled by your love and care.

Tom would like to thank Steve Wheeler, a Booz & Company partner and friend, without whom there would have been no research project and hence no book; his partners and colleagues at Booz & Company; and his wife, Beth, who patiently indulged him in this endeavor.

Ed is grateful for the love, understanding, and support of his wife, Patty.

All three of us would like to acknowledge Jim O'Toole, who provided encouragement and guidance through the project, and graciously agreed to write the foreword.

Last, we wish to express our appreciation to the members of the Center of Effective Organizations (CEO) at USC for their help and support of this project. A special word of thanks is extended to Alice Mark and Aaron Griffith for their technical, statistical, and creative support.

INDEX

Page references followed by *e* indicate an exhibit.

A

Abbott Laboratories, 15*e*

Absorptive capacity, 66

Accounting profitability metric, 8

Adaptability skills: of agile organizations, 56–57; comparing adapting and becoming adaptable, 56, 57. *See also* Change

Affordable Care Act of 2010 ("Obamacare"), 115, 122

After Action Reviews (AAR Process) [Harley-Davidson], 135

Aggressiveness: launching a price war as strategic, 63; Nokia's strategy market positioning dimension of, 60–61

Agile organizations: ability to change by, 98, 115; adaptability of, 56; ambidextrous structures for using information, 69; awareness of external environment by, 58; and choosing not to exploit their environment, 142; focus on current operations and future business opportunities by, 69; identity and intent components of strategy of, 58–59; implementing routine and embedded change management capability of, 115; implementing routine of, 27*e*, 28, 47–50; leadership as critical organization capacity of, 103–104; management learning as part of the culture of, 112; perceiving routine of, 27*e*, 43–45, 58, 66–80, 81*e*; relying on their perceiving routine and interpretation of information by, 79; strategizing routine of, 27*e*, 29, 30, 40–43, 55–66, 80–81*e*; testing routine of, 27*e*, 28, 45–47; top management teams (TMTs) of, 58, 62–64. *See also* Organizations

Agility: Agility Pyramid of, 28*e*–34; competitive advantage of, 140–141; defining, 26–28; as good management reconsidered, 34, 35*e*; introduction to four routines of, 27*e*–28; ITSS principle as foundation of capability for, 50–51, 114, 115, 126, 135; Johnson Controls (JCI) story on, 25–26; as level of Agility Pyramid, 28*e*, 31; organization development (OD) learning to focus on, 144–145; outputs of tests as the sine qua non of, 85; population ecology implications for, 32–33, 139; resource-based view of strategy,

29, 30, 139; sustainability potential of, 141–142; "West Coast offense" equivalent of, 140. *See also* Transforming to agility

Agility factor: as ability for rapid adaptation to the environment by a company, 18–19; Darwinian selection argument on, 12–14; description and characteristics of, 19; dynamic capabilities argument on the, 16–18; organizational physics argument on the, 14–16; organizing for, 25–52e; studies and theories offered on the, 11–12. *See also* Sustained performance

Agility profile scores: DaVita, 51e; Nokia, 81e; Zip Brands (hypothetical), 93e

Agility Pyramid: agility level of, 28e, 31; capabilities level of, 28e, 29; description of, 28–29; good management level of, 28e–29; illustrated diagram of, 28e; and implications for organization development, 31, 33–34

Agility routines: facilitating transformation by building, 114–115; implementing, 27e, 28, 47–50, 94–109; perceiving, 27e, 43–45, 66–80, 81e, 88–89; strategizing, 27e, 29, 30, 40–43, 55–66, 80–81e, 88–89; testing, 27e, 28, 45–47, 83–94, 134

Allstate Insurance Company: accelerating change through large group interventions (LGIs) at, 125–127; challenge leadership and clarifying strategy at, 125; COMPASS document on purpose, strategy, and values at, 125; examining the transformation process at, 115,

123–125; reflections on the transformation process at, 129–130; sustaining change and learning through LGIs at, 127–129; two objectives of transformation at, 124

Amazon: comparison of cumulative total shareholder returns (TSRs) of Microsoft, ExxonMobil, and, 7e; cumulative total shareholder returns of, 5, 6e; uncertain market environment during early days of, 13

American Express, 15e

American Machinery and Foundry (AMF), 130

American Research and Development Corporation, 1

Analyzed annual ROA (annual net income/total assets), 9, 10

Anderson, Harlan, 1

Andrews, Ken, 58–59

Apple: aggressiveness of, 80; "hip" image and iPhone technology advantage of, 54; initial market advantage enjoyed by, 12; organizational capability of, 30; thrasher performance pattern of, 18; uncertain market environment during early days of, 13

AT&T, 108

Auto industry performance, 131e

B

Bacon, Francis, 25

Ballmer, Steve, 94

Beals, Vaughn, 131

Beer, Michael, 72

Bennis, Warren, 34, 72

Berkshire Hathaway, 10

Bethlehem Steel, 29

Blockbuster, 95–96

Blue Cross Blue Shield, 116

Boeing, 15e, 16

Borders, 29

Bossidy, Larry, 94

Breadth: attacking new customer segment as strategic, 63; Nokia's strategy market positioning dimension of, 60

British Petroleum (BP), 18

Buckley, George, 61–62

Buell motorcycles, 136

Built to Last (Collins), 14

Built to Last companies, 14, 15*e*, 18

Burgelman, Robert, 72

C

Cambia Health Solutions: "The Cause" statement of strategic intent by, 116–117, 121, 122, 123; deliberate and insightful change process at, 119; designing and implementing the initiatives for change at, 118–121; examining the transformation process of, 115–117; Excellence in Leadership Award of, 120; fixing the foundation for transforming to agility, 115; initiating the identity journey of, 117–118; online training and SMART objectives used at, 120; plan-do-check-act cycle used at, 122; reflections on transformation of, 121–123

Camorra crime syndicate (Naples), 141

Campbell, John, 132

Campbell's Soup, 18, 141

Capabilities: companies with organizational, 30; definition of organizational, 30; dynamic, 16–18, 30; Netflix's change, 98, 105–109; ordinary, 30; 3M initiatives to restore innovation, 61–62

Capability development: agile organization approach to change management and, 98, 115; DaVita's agility building and, 39–50, 64–65; evolution of Netflix's, 107*e;* ITSS principle as foundation of, 50–51, 114, 115, 126, 135; learning as central to building, 109; need for organization development (OD) focus on, 144–145

Capital One: origins of, 83; "test and learn" at, 83–84, 87

Caviga, 136

Center for Effective Organizations (USC), 116

Chaltiel, Victor, 36, 37

Change: adapting versus becoming adaptable to, 56–57; agile organization's ability to, 98; Allstate's ability to learn and sustain, 127–129; crisis and change in identity required for, 64; ensuring delivery of expected results of, 96*e*; implementation embedded into an organization as full-scale, 107; implementing as well managed, 94–95; managing implementation of, 96*e*; Netflix's capability for, 98, 105–109; odds against strategic, 63; "unpopped kernel" problem of failed, 128. *See also* Adaptability skills; Transforming to agility

Change capability: learning as central part of building, 109; Netflix's, 98, 105–109; sustained performance driven by, 105

"Change fatigue," 17

Charan, Ram, 94

Christensen, Clayton, 12

Circuit City, 15*e*, 29

Citicorp, 15*e*

Clinton universal health care initiative (early 1990s), 115

Coldwell Banker real estate, 123

Collins, Jim, 14

Comcast, 108

Communication: of environmental information to decision makers, 67*e*, 71–78; interpreting environment signals as part of, 67*e*, 78–80; Nokia's internal "YouTube" SocialCast system and other paths of, 72, 73*e*, 74; portfolio of future scenarios element of, 75–78

Compaq, 2, 3

Competitive advantage: of agility, 140–141; Darwinian selection argument on, 12–13; dynamic capabilities as source of, 30; "hypercompetition" on limits of, 13; resource-based view of, 29, 30, 139

Core values: DaVita (DaVita HealthCare Partners), 58*e*; Nokia's emerging new, 65; of Zip Brands (hypothetical), 89*e*

Corporations. *See* Organizations

CPM operating system, 13

Cranz, Tawni, 102–104

"Culture of candor," 34

Customers: Allstate's transformation and improved service to, 129–130; attacking a new segment of, 63; Harley-Davidson's close working relationships with, 133; Netflix's economic logic used to serve, 96–97; Netflix's failure to test price increase acceptance of, 98; transparency and feedback of, 104

D

Darwin, Charles, 140

Darwinian selection: organizational agility explained through, 12–14; on population ecology, 31, 32–33, 139; on processes of variation, selection, and retention, 139

Data General's NOVA machine, 2

D'Aveni, R., 13

DaVita (DaVita HealthCare Partners): agile routines and sustained performance at, 51*e*; agility scores at, 51*e*; background information on, 34; breaking out of their thrasher or underperformer pattern, 11; building agility at, 39–50; interpretation of information at, 78–79; ITSS principle ("It's the system, stupid") of, 50–51; mission and core values of, 38*e*; profitability pattern of, 50–51, 52*e*; transformation of, 37–39. *See also* Thiry, Kent

DaVita agility building: events launching, 64–65; examining the process of, 39; implementing change, 47–50; perceiving environmental change, 43–45; strategizing dynamically for, 40–43; testing responses, 45–47

De Pree, Max, 58

Dean Witter Reynolds investments, 123

Decision makers: communicating environmental information to, 67*e*, 71–78; transparent vertical and horizontal channels to, 72

Differentiation: good management support of, 34; Nokia's strategy market positioning dimension of, 61

Digital Computer Corporation, 1

Digital Equipment Corporation (DEC), 1–2, 3, 14, 17, 64

Discover credit card, 123

Dodd-Frank Wall Street Reform and Consumer Protection Act, 141

Doriot, Georges, 1

DuPont, 2

Dynamic capabilities: organizational agility explained through, 16–18; as source of competitive advantage, 30

E
Eaton, 10
eBay, 12
Elop, Steve, 59, 61, 74
End-stage renal disease (ESRD), 36
Environment: agile organization's choice not to exploit its, 142; the agility factor as rapid adaptation to, 18–19; communicating environmental information to decision makers, 67e, 71–78; interpreting signals from the, 67e, 78–80; learning from your, 66; perceiving routine determined by awareness of external, 58; sensing any changes in the, 67e, 69–71. *See also* Perceiving routine
Execution: as doing better what you already know, 95; greater risk of implementation compared to, 94
Experiments: running the test to learn from, 87e, 92–94; setting up the test for, 87e, 91–92; testing as the routine for using and learning from, 86–87
ExxonMobil: adaptation to market environment by, 14; agility of, 141; comparison of cumulative TSRs of Microsoft, Amazon, and, 7e; cumulative total shareholder returns of, 6e; monthly total shareholder returns of, 5e

F
Facebook, 101
Fairbank, Rich, 83
Financial meltdown (2007), 84, 135, 141

Ford Motor, 2, 15e
Foster, Richard, 3–4
Fresenius Medical Care, 39

G
Galbraith's Star Model for organization design, 127
Gambro Healthcare, 39, 50–51
Ganz, Mark, 116, 117
Gap, Inc., 18, 142
GATT Uruguay Round (1986), 13
Gelb, Tom, 132
General Electric (GE): diversified organization of, 10; long-term longevity of, 2; organizational capability of, 30; strong development orientation of, 99
General Motors (GM), 13
Geneva Motor Show (2013), 136
Gerstner, Lou, 99–100
Geus, Arie de, 77
GlaxoSmithKline, 18
Global competition, during 1980, 13
Good management practices: agility as reconsideration of, 34, 35e; as Agility Pyramid level, 28e, 29; capabilities-based, 29, 31; differentiation supported by, 34; resource-based, 29, 30, 139; of survivor, thrasher, and outperformer organizations, 35e. *See also* Top management teams (TMTs)
Good to Great (Collins), 7, 14
Good to Great companies, 14, 15e, 18
Google, 1
Great Recession (2008–2009), 84, 135
Grove, Andy, 94

H
Harley Owners Group (HOG), 131, 134
"Harley Tariff" (1983), 131

Harley-Davidson (H-D): After Action Reviews (AAR Process) adopted at, 135; agility of, 141; auto industry performance rates of, 131e; Awareness Expansion (AE) workshops run by, 134; breaking out of thrasher or underperforming pattern, 11; Buell motorcycles acquired by, 136; customer relationships at, 133; events launching transformation to agility by, 64–65; examining the transformation process at, 130–131; Harley Owners Group (HOG) formed by, 131, 134; "Harley Tariff" (1983) petitioned by, 131; ITSS principle ("It's the system, stupid") adopted at, 135; "Joint Vision Process" to transform identity at, 132, 133; longevity enjoyed by, 2; MV August purchased by, 136; Performance Effectiveness Process (PEP) of, 133; Project Rushmore of, 133; recession's (2008–2009) impact on, 135; shared leadership and accountability driving transformation at, 132; slack resource investment made by, 134; "The Street" motorcycles introduced by, 136–137; testing done by, 134
Harley-Davidson Financial Services (HDFS), 132
Harley-Davidson Leadership Institute, 134
Harley-Davidson University (HDU), 134
Hastings, Reed, 97, 98
Hemingway, Ernest, 1
Herman Miller, 58
Hewlett-Packard, 1, 2, 15e
Holiday Corporation, 10

Holiday Rambler, 132, 136
Holmes, Oliver Wendell, 139
House of Cards series (Netflix), 98
Hudson Institute, 76
"Hypercompetition," 13

I
IBM: antitrust investigation of, 13; breaking out of its thrasher or underperformer pattern, 11; DEC as second only to (1990), 2; Jamming technology used by Nokia's global chat room, 65; Lou Gerstner's transformation of, 99–100; market performance (1980–2012) of, 15e; shift from mainframe computing by, 64; thrasher performance pattern of, 18
Identity (organizational): crisis as typically preceding change in, 64; description of, 59; Harley-Davison's "Joint Vision Process" to transform, 132, 133; Cambia Health Solutions' initiating change in, 117–118; ITSS principle ("It's the system, stupid") for managing change of, 115; Nokia's "Connecting People" mission and, 60, 65–66; perceiving routine features as reflection of, 67–68; setting transformation strategy by embedded change-friendly, 113–114; strategy as consisting of intent and, 58–59; sustainability embedded in Nokia's, 142
Implementing routine: comparing execution and, 94–95; DaVita's agility score on, 51e; DaVita's agility building through change, 47–50; description of, 27e, 28; ensuring delivery of expected results element of, 96e; as

full-scale change embedded into an organization, 107; managing implementation of the change element of, 96e; at Netflix, 95–109; Nokia's agility score on, 81e; as well-managed change, 94–95; Zip Brands (hypothetical) agility score on, 93e

In Search of Excellence (Peters and Waterman), 14

Industry/industries: managerial investment for growth within their, 8; McGahan's use of SIC industry to define, 9; North American Industry Classification System (NAICS), 10; "winner take all" dynamic of some types of, 13; within-industry change affecting, 13–14

Information: absorptive capacity to acquire and exploit, 66; ambidextrous structures of agile organizations for using, 69; communicated to decision makers, 67e, 71–78; interpreting environmental signals and, 67e, 78–80; taking action by using the most relevant, 106–107. *See also* Testing routine

Ingersoll-Rand, 10

Innovation: as result of a disciplined process, 86–87; testing as well-managed risk and, 86–87; testing tension between efficiency and, 90–91; 3M "15 percent rule" to encourage, 84–85; 3M initiatives to restore their capability for, 61–62

The Innovator's Dilemma (Christensen), 12

Intent (organizational): Cambia Health Solutions' "The Cause" statement of strategic, 116–117, 121, 122, 123; description of, 60; Nokia's "develop the ecosystem,"

61; strategy as consisting of identity and, 58–59; sustainability embedded in Nokia's, 142

ITSS principle ("It's the system, stupid"): Allstate's large group interventions (LGIs) for application of, 126; DaVita's use of the, 50–51; as foundation of the agile capability, 114; Harley-Davison's comprehensive approach to, 135; management of identity change by using, 115

J

Johnson & Johnson, 15e, 16, 18
Johnson Controls (JCI), 25–26

K

Kahn, Herman, 76
Kallasvuo, Olli-Pekka, 61, 65
Kaplan, Sarah, 3–4
Kimberly-Clark, 15e, 16
Kodak's talent management, 99–100
Kroger, 15e
Kubrick, Stanley, 76

L

Lamarck, Jean-Baptiste, 140
Large group interventions (LGIs): allowing a systematic approach to transformation, 126; Allstate's accelerated change through, 125–127; Allstate's sustained change and learning through, 127–129

Leadership: as critical organization capacity, 103–104; Harley-Davidson Leadership Institute for training, 134; Harley-Davidson's shared, 132; Netflix's shared, 102. *See also* Management; Top management teams (TMTs)

Learning: Allstate Insurance
Company story on sustaining
change and, 127–129; as central
to building change capability,
109; as part of the culture of
agile organizations, 112; running
the experimental test for, 87e,
92–94; testing as the routine for
using information and, 86–87;
3M's success due to captured, 92

M

Management: capabilities-based, 29,
31; good management practices,
28e, 29–31, 34, 35e, 139;
Harley-Davidson's Awareness
Expansion (AE) workshops run
for, 134; limited ability to adapt
to new requirements by, 32–33;
resource-based, 29, 30, 139;
talent, 98–102, 104–105.
See also Leadership; Top
management teams (TMTs)
Managing strategy execution:
description of, 62; strategizing
routine component of, 57e; TMT
(top management team) role in,
62–64
Market: S&P 500 stock index
benchmark for the, 3; total
shareholder return (TSR)
preference metric of the, 3
Marriott, 15e
McGahan, Anita, 8–9, 10
McGahan's performance data, 8e–9,
10–11
McGregor, Douglas, 143
McNerney, James, 61
Medicaid, 141–142
Medical Ambulatory Care, 36
Medicare, 141–142
Mello, Joe, 37, 47, 48
Merck, 15e
Microsoft: change management at,
94; comparison of cumulative

TSRs of Amazon, ExxonMobil,
and, 7e; initial market advantage
enjoyed by, 12; Nokia's mobile
devices business sold (2013)
to, 55; uncertain market
environment during early days
of, 13
Mintzberg, Henry, 60
Mission: DaVita (DaVita
HealthCare Partners), 58e;
Nokia's "Connecting People"
identity and, 60, 65–66;
perceiving routine features as
reflection of, 67–68
Modern Healthcare, 36
Morris, Nigel, 83
Motorola, 13, 15e, 53
MV August, 136

N

Napoleon, B., 11
National Medical Enterprises
(NME, now Tenet Healthcare),
36
Netflix: ability to implement major
changes by, 98, 105–109;
alignment and transparency
of, 102–104; background
information on, 95;
compensation approach taken by,
104–105; competition between
Blockbuster and, 95–96; context
and CDNs (content delivery
networks) of, 102–104, 108–109;
economic logic used to serve
customers by, 96–97; evolution
of capabilities of, 107e; failure to
test customer acceptance of
change in terms, 98; negative
public reaction to price increase
(2011) by, 97–98; Open Connect
distribution network of, 98;
shared leadership approach at,
102; talent management and
leadership at, 98–99, 101–102

Nokia: ability to sense environmental change at, 70–71, 80–81; "adaptive short-term planning" process used by, 64, 71–72, 74; agility scores of, 81*e*; ambidexterity and surface organizational designs of, 70, 71; Blog-Hub intranet soapbox at, 74; brand reputation of, 59–60; "Connecting People" identity and mission of, 60, 65–66; "develop the ecosystem" intent of, 61; dominance and expansion (1998–2007), 13, 53–54; history of organizational structures of, 73*e*; interpretation of information at, 71–72, 74–75, 77–78; internal "YouTube" SocialCast system and other communication paths at, 72, 73*e*, 74; mandate of Nokia Research Center (NRC), 70; mobile devices business sold to Microsoft (2013) by, 55; NAVTEQ acquired by, 53, 56; Nokia Open Studio project at, 75, 77–78; organization (2011–2012) by, 55*e*; Ovi Store of, 54; perceiving routines of, 68; ROA performance (1994–2009), 54*e*; strategizing to regain global market share, 55–56, 58–61; strategy market positioning dimensions of, 60–61; sustainability embedded in strategic intent and identity of, 142; "World Café" discussion groups and new values pushed by, 65

Nokia Research Center (NRC), 70

Nokia's top management teams (TMTs): "adaptive short-term planning" process used by, 64, 71–72, 74; interpretation of information by, 71–72, 74–75, 77–78; managing strategy execution role of, 57*e*, 62–64; revised set of values recommended by, 65

Nordstrom, 15*e*

North American Industry Classification System (NAICS), 10

NOVA machine (Data General), 2

Nucor, 15*e*, 16

O

"Obamacare" (Patient Protection and Affordable Care Act of 2010), 115, 122, 141

Olsen, Ken, 1, 2

OPEC oil embargo (1973), 76

Open Studio project (Nokia), 75, 77–78

Orange, 108

Ordinary capabilities, 30

Organization development (OD): emergence and development of, 143; as lacking in agility, 143; need for focus on agility to be effective, 144; professional division within, 143–144

Organization development (OD) practitioners: learning to focus on agility and capability development, 144–145; professional division among, 143–144

Organizational agility. *See* Agility

Organizational ecology, 31, 32–33

Organizational Learning Center (OLC) [MIT], 134

Organizational physics argument, 14–16

Organizations: *Built to Last* companies, 14, 15*e*, 18; *Good to Great* companies, 14, 15*e*, 18; identity component of strategy of, 58–60, 64–66, 113–118, 132, 133, 142; intent component of strategy by, 58–61, 116–117,

121, 122, 123, 142; life cycle of,
139; outperformer, 35e;
surviving versus thriving, 2–11;
survivor, 35e; U.S. Fortune 500
retention rates, 3e. See also
Agile organizations; Thrasher
organizations
O'Toole, James, 34, 72
Outperformer organization
management practices, 35e

P
Palmisano, Sam, 64
Pasteur, Louis, 53, 86–87
Patagonia, 142
Patient Protection and Affordable
Care Act of 2010
("Obamacare"), 115, 122, 141
PDP (Programmable Data
Processor), 1
PDP-11 computer (DEC), 2
Perceiving routine: DaVita's agility
score on, 51e; DaVita's agility
building through, 43–45;
description of, 27e, 66–67;
interaction and feedback between
strategizing and, 58; interpreting
environmental signals, 67e,
78–80; Nokia's agility score on,
81e; Nokia's successes and
failures of, 68; sensing the
environment element of the,
67e, 69–71; sensing without
communicating is waste, 67e,
71–78; testing as complementing
the, 88–89; Zip Brands
(hypothetical) agility score on,
93e. See also Environment
Performance: agility factor of
sustainable, 11–16; agility
potential for sustainable,
141–142; surviving versus
thriving, 2–11
Performance metrics: accounting
profitability, 8; analyzed annual
ROA (annual net income/total

assets), 9, 10; annual S&P 500
stock index rate of return, 3, 10;
McGahan's performance data,
8e–9, 10–11; total shareholder
return (TSR), 3–7e, 9, 10
Peters, Greg, 109
Peters, Thomas J., 14
Pfizer, 18
Philip Morris, 14, 15e
Pitney Bowes, 15e
Plan-do-check-act cycle, 122
Pollard, William, 83
Population ecology, 31, 32–33,
139
Porter, Michael, 63
Procter & Gamble: market
performance (1980 to 2012) of,
15e; organizational capability of,
30; organization development
(OD) impressive results at, 143;
as thrasher organization, 18
Project Rushmore (Harley-
Davidson), 133
Publilius Syrus, 111

Q
Qwikster, 97, 98

R
RAND Corporation, 76
Regence: background information
on, 116; new corporate vision
(2004) of, 116
"Regulatory capture," 142
Renal Care Group, 39
Renal Treatment Centers, 36, 37
Resources: expanded definition of,
30; resource-based view (RBV)
of management, 29, 30, 139;
slack resources investment to
rapidly deploy capable, 134;
valuable, rare, inimitable, and
nonsubstitutable (VRIN), 30
R.H. Donnelly, 29
Risk: extensive planning as often
futile attempt to control, 106; of

implementation compared to execution, 94; innovation and testing as well-managed, 86–87; tests as "low-cost probes" to help manage, 106–107

Royal Dutch Shell (RDS), 76–77

S

S&P 500 Stock Index: as performance metric, 3, 10; total shareholder return (1980 to 2012), 14, 15e, 16

Samsung, 53, 80

Sandberg, Sheryl, 101

SAP, 86

Sarbanes-Oxley regulations, 84

Scenarios: communication through portfolio of future, 75–78; history and development of, 76–77; Nokia Open Studio project, 75, 77–78

Sears Financial Network, 123

Senge, Peter, 134

Sensing: organization's abilities related to, 69; perceiving through environmental change, 67e, 69–71

Shared leadership approach: Harley-Davidson's use of the, 132; Netflix's use of the, 102

Shared responsibility philosophy, 34

Shareholder returns: Amazon cumulative total shareholder returns, 6e; comparison of Amazon, ExxonMobil, and Microsoft cumulative TSRs, 7e; ExxonMobil cumulative total shareholder returns, 6e; ExxonMobil monthly total shareholder returns, 5e; finance theory on, 4; total shareholder return (TSR) metric of, 3, 4–7

Siemens, 2

Simon, Herbert, 11

Six Sigma: identifying sources of waste as form of innovation, 86; 3M initiatives on using, 61

SMART objectives, 120

Smartphone market: Apple's and Google's "consumerization" of, 61; Nokia's dominance and expansion (1998–2007), 13, 53–54; Nokia's strategic market positioning in the, 60–61; Nokia's strategizing to regain global market share, 55–56, 61–62

Somma, Rande, 25–26

Sony, 15e

Sony Ericsson, 53

Soviet Union, 13

Standard Industrial Classification (SIC) system, 9, 10

Stimpson, Mark, 117, 118

Strategizing routine: DaVita's agility building through, 40–43; DaVita's agility score on, 51e; description of, 27e; developing the strategy element of, 57e, 58–62; establishing organizational purpose element of, 57e, 64–66; examples and images of, 56; interaction and feedback between perceiving and strategizing, 58; managing execution of the strategy element of, 57e, 62–64; Nokia's agility score on, 81e; Nokia's successful, 55–56, 58–61; resource-based view of, 29, 30, 139; testing as complementing, 88–89; 3M's successful, 61–62; Zip Brands (hypothetical) agility score on, 93e

Strategy: Allstate's challenge leadership and clarification of transformation, 125; developing the, 57e, 58–62; establishing organizational purpose of, 57e,

64–66; introducing identity and intent components of, 58–59; managing execution of the, 57e, 62–64; odds against successful change through, 63; setting a transformation, 113–114; as wasting asset that needs to be refreshed, 62

Survivor organization management practices, 35e

Sustained performance: agility and potential of, 141–142; change capability as driving, 105; Darwinian selection argument on, 12–14; a different way of defining, 9–11; dynamic capabilities argument on, 16–18; the old way of defining, 3–9; organizational physics argument on, 14–16; rapid environmental adaptation required for, 18–19. *See also* Agility factor

T

Talent management: IBM's successful, 99–100; Kodak's failed, 99–100; Netflix's above-market compensation as part of, 104–105; Netflix's successful, 98–99, 101–102; "travel light" approach to, 100

Teerlink, Rich, 131, 132, 133, 134, 135

Teller, Edward, 76

Testing routine: Capital One's, 83–84, 87; DaVita's agility score on, 51e; DaVita's agility building through, 45–47; description of, 27e, 28; Harley-Davidson's extensive, 134; learning from experiments, 87e, 92–94; as "low-cost probes" to help manage risk, 106–107; Netflix's failure to test customer acceptance, 98; Nokia's agility

score on, 81e; resourcing innovation and execution, 90–91; setting up and running experiments, 87e, 91–92; as the sine qua non of agility, 85; strategizing and perceiving complemented by, 88–89; as well-managed risk and innovation, 86–87; at Zip Brands, 87–94; Zip Brands (hypothetical) agility score on, 93e. *See also* Information

Thiry, Kent: on DaVita's implementation of change, 48, 49; on DaVita's mission, 40; on DaVita's testing responses, 45–47; on importance of accountability, 44, 46–47; "Murphy Team" led by, 47; promoting effective execution by his management team, 39; taking over as CEO at DaVita, 37; on value of nimbleness versus cost of chaos, 43, 46. *See also* DaVita (DaVita HealthCare Partners)

Thrasher organizations: adaptability without having agility characteristic of, 56–57; description of, 139; difficulty of interpreting environmental signals by, 80; good management practices of, 35e; IBM's breaking out of pattern of, 11; identity and intent components of strategy of, 58–59; performance pattern of, 18. *See also* Organizations

3M: captured learning component of success at, 92; "15 percent rule" at, 84–85; initiatives to restore innovation capabilities of, 61–62

Top management teams (TMTs): inability to monitor all aspects of organizations alone, 58; interpretation of information

essential to, 67*e*, 68, 78–80;
managing strategy execution role
of, 57*e*, 62–64; perceiving
routine as typically loosely
connected to, 66; perceiving
routine features as reflection of
strategic expectations of the,
68; revised set of values
recommended by, 65; setting the
strategy for transformation, 113.
See also Good management
practices; Leadership;
Management
Total Renal Care (TRC), 36–37
Total shareholder return (TSR):
Amazon cumulative, 6*e*; of *Build
to Last* and *Good to Great*
companies (1980 to 2012),
14, 15*e*; calculating, 4–5;
comparison of cumulative
Amazon, Microsoft, and
ExxonMobil, 7*e*; data from
1980 to 2012, 9; ExxonMobil
cumulative, 6*e*; ExxonMobil
monthly, 5*e*; as performance
benchmark, 4, 10; as preferred
performance metric, 3–4
Toyota: organizational capability of,
30; as thrasher organization, 18;
Toyota Production System of,
133
Transforming to agility: Allstate
Insurance Company story on,
115, 123–130; building agility
routines to facilitate, 114–115;
Cambia Health Solutions
story on, 115–123; fixing the
foundation to prepare for, 114,
115; Harley-Davidson (H-D)
story on, 130–137; having an
orientation to, 111–113; setting
the strategy for, 113–114. *See
also* Agility; Change
Transparency, 102–103, 104
TRW, 143

U
Uncertainty: extensive planning as
often futile attempt to control,
106; of implementation
compared to execution, 94;
innovation and testing as
well-managed risk and, 86–87;
tests as "low-cost probes" to help
manage, 106–107
United Technologies, 10
Universal health care: failure of
Clinton health care initiative
(early 1990s) for, 115;
"Obamacare" legislation working
toward, 115, 122, 141
UNIX operating system, 2
"Unpopped kernel" problem, 128
Uruguay Round (1986), 13
U.S. Fortune 500 retention rates, 3*e*
USA Today, 108

V
Valuable, rare, inimitable, and
nonsubstitutable (VRIN)
resources, 30
Vanjoki, Anssi, 53–54
VAX (Virtual Address eXtension)
computer [DEC], 2
Volcker, Paul, 13
Volvo, 143

W
Walgreens, 15*e*
Wal-Mart, 15*e*, 16
Wall Street Journal, 97
Walt Disney, 15*e*, 16
Wandell, Keith, 136
Waterman, Robert H., Jr., 14
Wells Fargo, 15*e*
What Really Works (Joyce, Nohria,
and Roberson), 7
"World Café" discussion groups, 65
World Trade Organization (WTO),
13
Wozniak, Steve, 2

Y
Yahoo, 13
Yom Kippur War, 76
YouTube, 109

Z
Zip Brands (hypothetical company):
   agility profile of, 93*e*;

background of, 87–88; core
values of, 89*e*; learning from
experiments at, 92–93;
resourcing innovation and
execution at, 90–91; setting
up and running experiments
at, 91–92; testing routine at,
87–94